BERNIE!
BERNIE!
BERNIE!

BERNIE!
BERNIE!
BERNIE!

by
BERNIE PARENT
with
BILL FLEISCHMAN
and
SONNY SCHWARTZ

Prentice-Hall, Inc., Englewood Cliffs, N.J.

Books by Sonny Schwartz:

CONFESSIONS OF A DIRTY
BALLPLAYER

SO LONG JOEY

ON GOD'S SQUAD: THE STORY
OF NORM EVANS

Design by Linda Huber

Bernie! by Bernie Parent with Bill Fleischman and Sonny Schwartz
Copyright © 1975 by Bernard M. Parent
All rights reserved. No part of this book may be
reproduced in any form or by any means, except
for the inclusion of brief quotations in a review,
without permission in writing from the publisher.
Printed in the United States of America
Prentice-Hall International, Inc., London
Prentice-Hall of Australia, Pty. Ltd., Sydney
Prentice-Hall of Canada, Ltd., Toronto
Prentice-Hall of India Private Ltd., New Delhi
Prentice-Hall of Japan, Inc., Tokyo

10 9 8 7 6 5 4 3 2 1

Library of Congress Cataloging in Publication Data

Parent, Bernie.
    Bernie!

     1. Parent, Bernie.   2. Hockey.
I. Fleischman, Bill.   II. Schwartz, Sonny.
III. Title.
GV848.5.P28A33   796.9'62'0924 [B]   75–38542
ISBN 0–13–074526–X

TO: My wife Carol, my children,
and the rest of my entire
family for all their love,
understanding, and guidance
over the years; and to each
coach and member of every
hockey team I ever played with
for helping me achieve the
success I have.

Season	Club	Lea
1965–66	Oklahoma City	CPHL
1965–66	Boston	NHL
1966–67	Boston	NHL
1966–67	Oklahoma City	CPHL
1967–68	Philadelphia	NHL
1968–69	Philadelphia	NHL
1969–70	Philadelphia	NHL
1970–71	Philadelphia	NHL
	Toronto	NHL
1971–72	Toronto	NHL
1972–73	Philadelphia **(e)**	WHA
1973–74	Philadelphia **(abc)**	NHL
1974–75	Philadelphia **(bcd)**	NHL

NHL Totals

BERNARD MARCEL PARENT

Born April 3, 1945, in Montreal
Goaltender   Height 5'11"   Weight 180
Last amateur club: Niagara Falls, OHA

Regular Schedule					Playoffs				
GPI	**MINS**	**GA**	**SO**	**AVE**	**GPI**	**MINS**	**GA**	**SO**	**AVE**
3		11	0	3.67					
39	2083	128	1	3.69					
18	1022	62	0	3.64					
14		37	*4	2.70					
38	2248	93	4	2.49	5	355	8	0	*1.35
58	3365	151	1	2.69	3	180	12	0	4.00
62	3680	171	3	2.79					
30	1586	73	2	2.76					
18	1040	46	1	2.65	4	235	9	0	2.30
47	2715	116	3	2.56	4	243	13	0	3.20
63	3653	220	2	3.61	1	70	3	0	2.57
73	4314	136	*12	*1.89	17	1042	35	*2	*2.02
68	4041	137	*12	*2.03	15	922	29	*4	*1.89
451	26094	1113	39	2.55	48	2977	106	6	2.13

*   *Led League*
a   *Shared Vezina Trophy with Tony Esposito*
b   *First All-Star team*
c   *Won Conn Smythe Trophy*
d   *Won Vezina Trophy*
e   *Second All-Star Team*

CONTENTS

FOREWORD

During my career in professional hockey I have seen and been associated with many great goaltenders. Turk Broda was with Toronto when I came up to the National Hockey League as a defenseman with the New York Rangers. Chuck Rayner was the Rangers' goalie. I have played against the great Bill Durnan and I coached Jacques Plante. But to me, Bernie Parent is the greatest of them all.

All goalies are under pressure, but who has been under more pressure than Bernie when he returned to the Philadelphia Flyers after a year in the new World Hockey Association? Bernie had left his WHA team, the Philadelphia Blazers, during the play-offs over a financial dispute. Now he was back in the NHL knowing people would examine his every move. Bernie could have fallen flat on his goalie's mask and been humiliated. Instead, he helped the Flyers win the Stanley Cup.

The year before, when Bernie was in the WHA, the Flyers had stunned many people by reaching the Stanley Cup semifinals against Montreal. We lost, but we knew we'd be back. Whether we could have won the cup without Bernie, I don't know, but with him in the nets we were able to gamble more. With another goalie it would be necessary to play tighter.

As hockey fans know, goalies are unique. They play the toughest position in sports, which affects these men differently.

Some are loners. They don't mix with the team and hardly go anywhere themselves. They're in a world by themselves.

Other goalies drink or eat too much. I knew one NHL goalie who needed a couple belts before he could play.

To keep the goalie happy, the coach would drink with him.

Those who eat too much do it because they are nervous. Some goalies are always complaining. The trainer isn't treating him right or his hotel room is too hot or his steak isn't cooked the way he likes it. With these complainers, all goals they allow are never their fault. It's always "a defenseman screened me" or "our winger let his man get away. What could I do?"

And other goalies act a little goofy. Doug Favell was our goalie when I came to Philadelphia. When he warmed up, he put on a Harlem Globetrotters' type show. He would catch pucks between his legs or make saves look harder than they were. The crowds loved him. They thought he was putting on a show, but actually his "show" was his way of covering up his nervousness.

Once, when we were driving to Philadelphia International Airport, I mentioned to Bernie that he didn't fit into one of the goalie categories I just described.

"No, Freddie," he said, smiling. "I fit into all of them."

The man's sense of humor is amazing. He really seems like one of the team. He goes everywhere with the players and enjoys life.

When Bernie played in the IVB Golf Classic Pro-Am tournament at Whitemarsh Valley Country Club last summer, he was paired with pro Ken Still. After the tournament Still told Ray Didinger of the Philadelphia *Evening Bulletin,* "Bernie has an unbelievable temperament for golf, the best I ever saw. He never gets upset."

I hope Bernie doesn't decide to try the pro golf tour for at least five more years. Incidentally, Bernie plays golf left-handed. And you know what they say about lefties. . . .

Despite his friendly nature, Bernie must hide some feelings. He never gets angry and he's always forgiving. He never denounces his own players. If we win, it's because the team did well. If we lose, he accepts the blame.

Before Keith Allen, the Flyers' general manager, and Ed Snider, the club's chairman of the board, approved the trade to bring Bernie back to the Flyers, they asked what I thought.

I asked who was better, Bernie or Doug Favell? Keith said Bernie was better, but he was worried about the Philadelphia fans' reaction because Favell was a colorful, popular goalie.

"The hell with the fans," I said. "If Bernie is the best, the fans will accept him."

When Bernie reported for training camp, I really didn't know what to expect. I had only seen him play a few times. In the Central League our team had beaten him the three times he faced us. Once we won by something like eight goals, but when I thought about it, I realized each goal was a good one. The Blazers weren't a fair test for him because his team was basically inexperienced and the league was wide open.

We didn't talk much at camp. I didn't want him thinking I was nervous about how he would do.

After his first exhibition game with us, I could have been a nervous wreck. The Rangers scored seven goals in twenty-two minutes against him at the Spectrum, and many fans booed. All he did was shrug it off because he knew it was still early. At that moment I knew I had the greatest goalie in the world.

Now that Bernie and Bobby Clarke have contracts that guarantee them financial security for life, many people have asked if I think their play will be affected.

There are athletes who sign long-term contracts

13

and then let up a little. They figure, "Why kill myself? I know I'll be with this club a long time."

I don't think Bernie or Bobby will develop such an attitude. If either of them were digging sewers or working as carpenter's helpers, they'd work just as hard.

They are special people and the Flyers are fortunate to have them.

Fred Shero

Philadelphia

BERNIE!
BERNIE!
BERNIE!

THE
1975
STANLEY
CUP
FINALS

Carrying that cup around the ice is the dream of every Canadian boy.

Sitting around a hotel swimming pool in a short-sleeved shirt and seeing girls in bikinis isn't the best way to concentrate on a hockey game. Especially a Stanley Cup final game.

But the Flyers hadn't come this far to let warm weather and pretty scenery distract them. We were one win from our second straight Stanley Cup and were determined to prove we weren't just a bunch of "animals," as our critics called us. If we could beat Buffalo in the sixth game—in their building—we were sure people would finally agree we deserved to be champions.

Even though we tried not to think about it much, the scene in Buffalo was strange. The Indianapolis 500, the auto race that is always held on Memorial Day weekend, had been run, but the Stanley Cup finals, the conclusion of a winter sport, still weren't over. The finals had run late before, into mid-May, when it gets hot. But this was crazy. We had to play on May 27, 1975, the latest the play-offs had ever gone. Usually by this time hockey players are vacationing in Florida.

Our first play-off trip to Buffalo had been memorable because of the "fog" game. We had won the first two games of the best-of-seven series in Philadelphia, by 4–1 and 2–1, so Buffalo almost had to win its first home game. When the game started, the temperature outside was in the high 70s. Inside, it must have been 90°. On the ice it felt 110°, and inside the mask at least 130°.

Early in the game, fog started rising from the ice. The mist wasn't too bad until about midway in the game.

The fog couldn't be dissipated because Buffalo's building isn't air-conditioned. So we had to stop the game every few minutes and have players from both teams skate around trying to circulate the air. Like our captain, Bobby Clarke, said later, it looked pretty bush for the league. Buffalo's solution to clearing the fog in the next game was to bring out some kids waving white sheets. I guess it looked funny, unless you were playing. The whole thing was a shame and looked bad for the league. I think the NHL should have a rule that every building be air-conditioned. The games mean too much to be decided by a fluke goal through the fog. Besides, both teams were lucky nobody got hurt.

The only crazy thing connected with the fog was that right about that time I got new radar equipment for my thirty-three-foot boat. I could have used radar that night in Buffalo. Trying to stop shots by Buffalo's "French Connection Line" is hard enough under normal conditions. Having them wear white sweaters and shoot at you through the fog is a good way to go into early retirement. Or the hospital.

Anyway, they beat us 5–4 in overtime on René Robert's goal. They also won the next game, 4–2, and then we went back to the Spectrum and won easier than most people expected, 5–1. Dave Schultz's goal from deep on the left side a little over three minutes into the game deflected in past their goalie, Gerry Desjardins, and we were on our way.

On our first trip to Buffalo during the finals, we stayed at the Sheraton East, near the airport. It's a nice hotel, with a partially enclosed swimming pool surrounded by tropical plants and cabana-style tables. The only problem was that many of our fans had arranged to stay at the hotel, so there was a party atmosphere during our stay.

Fred Shero, our coach, wants us to enjoy ourselves in the play-offs. He's not like some coaches who hide their teams. Hockey players like to have a good time as much as anyone, but they know the Stanley Cup finals are important and will avoid anything that might hurt their chances. Buffalo didn't even stay in Philadelphia between games three and four. Since it was the Sabres first Stanley Cup final, maybe their management thought the guys might get rattled. But hell, the year before when we played Boston in our first final, we didn't jump back and forth between games and we still won.

Coming back to Buffalo for the sixth game, Freddie Shero moved us to a hotel near Niagara Falls, the Holiday Inn at Grand Island. It was a good move. Only the team was there, no fans or writers. Unlike some teams, we've got a good bunch of writers who travel with us. They aren't always bothering us or snooping around away from the rink. They do their job, and do it well, but then they leave us alone. Usually the writers stay in the same hotel we do, but this time Freddie just wanted the team. No outsiders.

All our rooms faced the water, so we could sit out on our porches, have a cold beer, and watch the boats go by. It was a great way to relax, especially for me because I often think about my boat and going deep-sea fishing out of Wildwood, New Jersey. We keep the boat at the dock on the bay behind our summer home there.

Since we arrived at the hotel on Monday afternoon and were playing Tuesday night, I could go through my usual routine of preparation. The night before I always think about the next game, going over the shooters and how I'll have to stop them.

I'll usually go out, maybe have a couple drinks, eat a good dinner, then go back to my room, where I'll watch television and start thinking about the game. The next day I don't want to even think about hockey until I have to. After we beat Buffalo, the writers asked if I dream about stopping shots.

"What do you want me to do," I asked, "get tired *before* the game?"

If a goaltender gets too tight or nervous before a game, he'll be tight on the ice and make mistakes. He won't do the right things because he'll hesitate.

Going into the final game against Buffalo, I thought we had a little edge because from what we read and heard, their goalies, Desjardins and Roger Crozier, didn't sound anxious to play.

Desjardins is a guy about my age who had started the season in the World Hockey Association. When the Michigan team moved to Baltimore, Desjardins was able to get out of his contract. Buffalo made a deal with the New York Islanders for his NHL rights, and for the last month of the season he really played well. Desjardins also helped Buffalo beat Chicago and Montreal in the play-offs, but he had a couple shaky games in our series, like the one in Philly where Schultzie's shot got past him.

Crozier had been around a long time. He won the Conn Smythe Trophy in 1966 when his Detroit team lost to Montreal in the finals. The last couple years, though, Crozier had stomach troubles, and I don't think Buffalo knew when they could count on him. But Crozier was the type who could come up real strong for four or five games, so we were a little worried about how he would play.

Crozier did play well, but we got the breaks. We didn't get the breaks until the third period, but getting them is what counts.

There was no score after two periods. I knew then that the team scoring the first goal would win. That's what usually happens in a scoreless hockey game. When both teams have worked hard for a long time, the team that gives up the first goal suddenly feels as if it has been hit in the stomach by Joe Frazier. It's discouraging. You tell yourself not to give up, to fight back, but it's hard to do.

It was hot again for the game, but once the game starts you're concentrating so much you forget about the heat. Everybody is in top shape by that time of the season. After the overtime game we played against Buffalo, everybody was tired. But by the next morning we all felt fine.

The Sabres made me work hard in that final game. They have a very talented team. The French Connection Line of Gil Perreault, Richard Martin, and René Robert is tough to stop for sixty minutes. But people often overlook their other players, guys like Don Luce, Craig Ramsay, Danny Gare, Jim Lorentz, and Brian Spencer. A lot of people thought Luce's line was Buffalo's best in the play-offs, with Ramsay their club's top Conn Smythe Trophy candidate. And that Spencer will do anything to help his team win. As soon as the Sabres straighten out their goaltending and get more experience on defense, they'll be dynamite.

They were really something for the first two periods. I had to make big saves on Robert and Jocelyn Guevremont in the first period. Geez, that Guevremont had a tough series. He has a great shot from the point, but I noticed after the finals that he was 0 for 53 shooting for the entire play-offs.

The toughest stretch of the game was in the second period. Somebody told me later I made six saves in about three minutes. They were shooting from everywhere: Perreault from the right, Robert from about twenty feet, Rick Dudley from right in front. I had to use everything—my stick, glove, arms—to keep the puck out of the net. A couple times our defensemen cleared loose pucks from near the goal line. Once, Moose Dupont, our big defenseman, had a head-lock on Lorentz, but the referee, Bruce Hood, didn't call a penalty. The crowd got on Hood, but, like I said, we got the breaks.

With the score 0–0 against Buffalo, after two periods we were still confident. Freddie has taught us to keep working and not to look too far ahead. We just go from one face-off to the next face-off, from one period to the next. Worry about what will happen two periods from now and you're in trouble. We get in this habit during the season and it carries over to the play-offs.

Some might say Bob Kelly is the last guy you'd expect to score the winning goal in a Stanley Cup final, but it was the "Hound" who did it. Kelly scored only eleven goals all season. He doesn't even take a regular shift, but he's another example of what makes our team go.

Guys like Kelly are why we've won two Stanley Cups in a row and will be in contention for a long time. On our team, everybody is as important as everybody else. Some are mainly checkers, but, like Don Saleski, what they do is as important as Reggie Leach or Rick MacLeish scoring goals.

Sure, we have leaders like Bobby Clarke, but there

are no really big stars. Look what happened when I got hurt before the Islanders' semifinal series. Wayne Stephenson, who played in only twelve games all season, came in and won two straight games. He even shut out the Islanders in the opener.

When we beat the Bruins for the Stanley Cup in 1974, some thought it was a fluke. They didn't think we were that good. Well, anytime you shut out the Bruins 1–0 in a Stanley Cup final game, it's no fluke. I had a good game, but I had a lot of help. To me, our success has been proof that a good team will beat a team that depends on a couple of individuals. Bobby Orr and Phil Esposito are great players, but they haven't been able to bring Boston the cup for two straight years. As great as the Bruins have been with Orr and Esposito, we've done something they've never done—win back-to-back Stanley Cups.

Now Kelly has his name in the record book next to Orr, Jean Béliveau, Henri Richard, and others for scoring the game-winner in a Stanley Cup final. I think it's great for Kelly. It's something he'll never forget. And the way he scored was typical of our team. Clarkie, who weighs about 180 pounds, bumped Jerry Korab, Buffalo's 215-pound defenseman, behind the net and got the puck to the Hound, who slid it past Crozier only eleven seconds after the period began.

Seeing Kelly out there to start the period surprised some, but Mike Nykoluk, our assistant coach, had suggested using him. Freddie is always willing to listen to Mike and Barry Ashbee, our other assistant coach. Of course, when you're in a scoreless game, you're willing to try anything.

The Hound always stirs things up for us. Even

though he doesn't score many goals, our fans at the Spectrum love the Hound for the way he roams around crashing into people.

A 1–0 lead over the Sabres isn't too safe, but I had a good feeling. I think they had gotten a little discouraged by not scoring earlier. I know one time Guevremont seemed to have an open corner of the net, but I got my arm up at the last second and deflected the puck. I could see Guevremont shaking his head as he skated away.

Buffalo's last good scoring chance came with a little over three minutes left to play. Luce got off a twenty-five-footer from the slot, but I stopped it. Then Orest Kindrachuk and Bill Clement, two more guys who weren't among our top scorers, combined to get the insurance goal. Kindrachuk, whom we call "O" so we don't take five minutes pronouncing his name, got the puck to Clement, even though Korab was about to send "O" into the boards. "I watched the goal from the fifth row of seats," Kindrachuk said.

Billy scored his first goal of the play-offs with 2:43 to go, and we had a 2–0 win and the cup. That goal was Billy's last as a Flyer because a week after the season he was the key man in a trade with Washington.

When the play-offs are finally over, you don't have time to think about the pressure being off. The players are hugging and congratulating each other, then you line up to shake hands with the other team. To me, this handshaking tradition is one of the classiest things in sports. It's like seeing two heavyweights who've been pounding each other for fifteen rounds stopping to show how much they respect each other.

And then Clarence Campbell, the National Hockey

League president, is on the ice with the cup. What a great sight! They tell me the cup cost only about fifty dollars when it was purchased by Lord Stanley in 1893. Well, to any player who is on a Stanley Cup winner, that gleaming silver trophy is priceless. Knowing you helped win it and that your name will be engraved on it is an indescribable thrill.

We all get a nice check for winning the cup ($15,000) plus another $4,000 or so for winning our division, but I've never heard a Flyer mention the money. Maybe it's because we all make good salaries, but I think it's because we are all so proud of being part of a winner.

The Buffalo fans were good to us when the series had ended. I know they were proud of their team for giving it a great try. And I know they don't like us. But when Clarkie and I took the cup for the traditional skate around the ice, the fans applauded us and even chanted, "Ber-nie! Ber-nie! Ber-nie!" the way our fans in Philly do.

Taking that skate with the cup meant a lot to us because we didn't get the chance in Philly after we beat Boston in 1974. The fans jumped onto the Spectrum ice and mobbed us so much we could hardly move. Carrying the cup around the ice is the dream of every Canadian boy. The way things are now with women's rights, maybe even some Canadian girls are dreaming about it, too. But I don't think I'll still be playing if that day ever comes.

When we got to the cramped dressing room, it was a madhouse. People and champagne were everywhere. Al Meltzer, sports director of Channel 3 in

Philadelphia, was there with his camera crew. I found out that I had won the Conn Smythe Trophy again. The trophy goes to the most valuable player on his team for the play-offs. It's nice knowing I'm the first back-to-back winner, but I don't know how the writers could single out any one of our players. I'm glad I didn't have to vote.

The next day, there was an unbelievable parade in Philadelphia to honor us. After we beat Boston, a couple hundred thousand people were expected. Instead, the crowd was estimated at a couple million. I'll never forget the sight of looking out over Independence Mall and seeing wall-to-wall people.

I wish I were smart enough to understand why the people in Philly like us so much. I know they hadn't had a winning professional team for a long time until we won the first cup. Everybody loves a winner, but here we are—a bunch of Canadians—who have become almost part of the family to millions of Philadelphians. Some fans even came up with a bumper sticker: "Only the Lord Saves More Than Bernie Parent."

All I know is their support helps keep us going. Nobody likes us when we go into Boston or New York or L.A. I guess many of those fans even hate us because we are a rough team. But we always know that when we come back home we'll be cheered. There's a real warmth between the Flyers and their fans, and I hope it never stops.

The parade after we beat Buffalo was better organized because the city knew what to expect. This time we were riding on flatbed trucks, where the fans could see us but not touch us. The year before, we were in convertible cars and the crowd got too close. Clarkie had to go back to the Spectrum because people were grabbing him. Cans and bottles almost hit him and other players.

We had been up all night after returning from Buffalo and had had a few beers. The only thing the city didn't provide on those trucks was johns. Nature's call finally got so unbearable that they stopped the truck on South Broad Street, a policeman who was escorting us handcuffed himself to me, and we knocked on a door so I could use the bathroom. Peter Chille of 1528 South Broad Street was a gracious "host." Later Ed Snider, our owner, said, "That might be the most publicized leak in history."

The parade ended at Kennedy Stadium, where the Army-Navy football game is played. Over 100,000 people were in the stands. Most of them had been there for hours, waiting for our caravan to arrive from center city. Many of the fans had been up celebrating all night, too.

When it was my turn to speak, I thanked the people for being there. When I said, "See you all here again next May twenty-eighth," the crowd roared.

I think Clarkie described the crowd and excitement best when he said:

"Maybe that's as close to heaven as we'll ever get."

GROWING UP— WITH HOCKEY

I have a brother who is a psychologist . . . just what every goaltender needs.

Before we could leave Buffalo we had to wait for our dressing room to empty. Then we dressed and left by bus for the Buffalo Airport.

Our chartered plane was crowded. Aboard were players, coaches, club officials and their wives and friends, writers, broadcasters, and friends and relatives of the players. Again, I was reminded of what a big family the Flyers have become. Several fathers of the players spend the entire play-offs with us. The father of Joe and Jimmy Watson; Dave Schultz's father; and the fathers of Bobby Clarke and Don Saleski have traveled with us. I think the parents' interest is just another example of our team's closeness.

Before the plane took off, Bob Dowd, the United Air Lines sports representative, walked back to where I was sitting and said there was a call for me in the cockpit. I had never been called in a plane before—I felt like President Ford or a big corporation executive.

When Dowd said it was my father calling to congratulate us from the tower at Philadelphia's airport where another huge crowd was waiting to welcome us home, I thought something was strange. As far as I knew, my dad, Claude, was in Montreal. I navigated my way through the congested plane aisle to the cockpit. As soon as I heard the man's voice, I knew it wasn't Claude. I said, "Thanks for calling," and put down the earphones. It must have been some nervy fan who managed to convince the airlines' brass that he was Claude.

As you would expect, the plane was a noisy place. The guys were drinking beer and yelling, but I noticed no one was too rowdy. That's another thing about the Flyers—we play rough on the ice, but I have never been embarrassed by the way the guys act off the ice. We don't raise hell on planes or in hotels. We confine that kind of behavior to the ice.

When I reached my seat, I looked around at the guys enjoying themselves. Joe Watson and Eddie Van Impe were needling each other, as they continually do. The Hound still had a big grin on his face. Teddy Harris, who had announced his retirement as an NHL player after playing on his fifth Stanley Cup winner, was laughing and talking with Ross Lonsberry. When Teddy, who was named coach of the Minnesota North Stars a few weeks later, was shaking hands with the players in the dressing room, his eyes were misty and he kept repeating, "What a way to go out."

I watched the whole scene for a few minutes, then closed my eyes. I just had to think for a while.

A few seconds passed before I said to myself, "Parent, you are a lucky so-and-so." My career has had more ups than downs, for which I'm very grateful, but there have been rough times. As I sat there, my thoughts returned to Montreal and the place where I grew up. Why I would think about Rosemont at a time like that I don't know. My best guess is, I was happy after beating Buffalo, I was happy in Rosemont, and I appreciate all the good things that have happened to me.

Rosemont is a section in East Montreal. It's a working man's neighborhood, far off the path of visitors who think of Montreal as only the Queen Elizabeth Hotel, the

Château Champlain Hotel, Les Filles du Roi Restaurant, and the Expo site. While Rosemont doesn't have fancy homes and large, lush green lawns, it's a nice area. The homes are neat, the streets are clean, and people care about each other.

It was in this atmosphere that I grew up. I was born April 3, 1945, at 1443 Cutareau Street. It wasn't an easy time for my parents. My mother, Emilie, was thirty-seven years old. My father, Claude, was forty-two. I was the youngest of seven children, and before I was born my mother had been ill with pneumonia.

After I was born, my mother wasn't strong enough to look after me around the clock so my sister Raymonde and cousin Denise took care of me. They tell me that I used to cry and cry. No wonder! I was starving! That's true. I wasn't getting enough to eat. Raymonde and Denise realized what was happening and soon had me on a diet that kept me happy.

I was too young to remember, but my family tells me that I used to suck my thumb. Many children do it, but I had to be different. I would put a piece of cotton between my forefinger and thumb, than suck my thumb and the cotton. To break this habit my mother tried soaking the cotton in vinegar. To her amazement, I liked the vinegar taste so much I asked for more. When I think about the combination of vinegar and cotton now, I want to gag.

Like every child, I had other odd habits. When I was three or four years old, I'd sit in the middle of the street playing and hold up my hand like a policeman as trucks came down the street. The trucks would stop, the drivers would get out, pick me up, and put me on the sidewalk.

If you read deeply into behavior like that, maybe I was showing then I could handle danger and eventually be a goaltender. I'll leave thinking like that to my brother Yvan. He is a child psychologist in Montreal where he lives with his wife, Michelle, and their children. When the Philadelphia hockey writers learned that I have a brother who is a psychologist, they broke up. Just what every goaltender needs, they said. They asked if I spoke often with him. I said, "Sure, *he* calls me once a week for advice."

So here was this brave youngster who defied two-ton trucks—a really tough kid, right? Well, I was also afraid of the dark. Some tough guy. Every night before going to bed, I would check under the bed, behind the doors, and in the cupboard. I don't know whom I expected to find. Maybe Bobby Hull ready to fire a slap-shot at me?

My father was a machine operator for Canada Cement Company. He was offered foreman's jobs, but didn't want the responsibility. Claude didn't make a lot of money, but we had enough to live well. I don't know how they managed, but my parents had enough money to send my brother Yvan, and my sisters Raymonde, Marie-Claude, and Thérèse to college. My brother Jacques and sister Louise decided not to attend college.

One way my mother helped was making our clothes. We didn't look fancy, right out of Eaton's Department Store, or Simpson's, but we had nice clothes. When you know your mother worked hard to make the clothes, you take better care of them.

We weren't able to take expensive vacations. Most of our visits were to relatives in Montreal and other parts of Quebec. I was interested mainly in sports anyway, so

I didn't know if I was missing anything. When you don't know what anything good is, you don't miss it.

When I was about ten years old, my parents bought a house at 1885 Bruxelles Street. It was near the house where I was born. Some people may think it's strange, but I don't remember that much about my younger years. Maybe the reason is I was so involved with sports that I sort of shut out everything else. Friends such as Bob Martineau and Mike Lemieux and I were so busy with football, baseball, and street hockey that we hardly had time for school.

I probably didn't realize it, but it was obvious in my early grades that I wouldn't be following my brothers and sisters to college. School just didn't interest me. It was my fault. My mother used to keep after me and so did the rest of the family, although except for Thérèse the other children were older and weren't around too much.

When I was in grade three at Boucher de la Bruère on Lepailleur Street, my sister Marie-Claude was my teacher. Such an arrangement was awkward for both of us. Marie-Claude had to be careful not to show favoritism and I didn't want to give her any trouble. I tried to behave in school. She said I wasn't a problem, but when I got home I completely avoided her.

I wasn't always an angel. What school-age child is? One time my mother took me to visit one of my sisters who was in a boarding school run by nuns. As we entered the school, a nun came out to greet my mother and me. When the nun bent down to say hello, I thought she was going to kiss me as adults did at home, so I reached up, threw my arms around her, and kissed her.

The nun was startled, but my mother tried to handle the situation calmly.

Another time, my mother took me to our church, Eglise St.-François d'Assise, on Notre-Dame Street. Mother gave me a nickel to put in the collection plate, but I hid the money. When the plate was passed to us, my mother noticed that I didn't put in the nickel. When we left church, she insisted I tell her what happened to the nickel. I wouldn't, so she started shaking me and I started crying. I don't think that candy bar was worth the trouble I went through.

Yvan and Jacques got me started playing hockey. They used to work with me in our backyard. I didn't start out to be a goalie, but they noticed that I had good balance. The balance, combined with the fact that I couldn't exactly skate like Rick MacLeish does now, convinced them I should be a goalie.

Yvan was coaching a bantam team whose goalie was injured in a car accident. We had talked around home about me being a goalie, so he asked if I would try it. I was about nine years old and had never been on skates to play hockey, but I agreed to put on the pads. Until then, I had only played on the streets wearing boots and shooting tennis balls.

The main thing I remember about that first experience in goal was I looked like a dumb ass. I felt clumsy wearing the goalie's equipment. I wasn't used to the gear, so trying to move in it was difficult. On the street we had tried to imitate Jacques Plante. With all the equipment on, it wasn't easy.

Somehow, I played okay. Things turned out well the rest of the season and we made the play-offs. The most memorable thing from the play-offs that year was being able to wear some pads a friend, Gilles Boutin, had gotten from his father. Gilles's pads first caught my eye because they were new—and red! For me, seeing those pads was just like a kid in the States see his friend get a new baseball glove. I really envied Gilles.

One night during the play-offs, Claude and Gilles's father were talking in our living room. Mr. Boutin turned to me and said, "Why don't you wear the red pads?"

I was hoping to hear that for a long time. I was excited. Being polite was the last thing I thought of. There was no "Well, gee, I'm not sure . . . maybe I'd better not." I quickly replied, "Yes, thank you, I will."

Well, old "big mouth" paid for his wish. The pads were too big as I discovered when I tried to move in warm-up that night. But I just had to wear them. Fortunately, we won the game. It was something like 16–15, but at least we won.

After those play-offs, I was hooked on playing goal. Actually, my future job was probably determined the first time I went in the nets in street hockey. I loved challenging the shooters.

"Come on," I'd yell, in French, "try to get it past me." When I'd make a stop, it was such a great feeling that I couldn't wait to stand up to the shooters again.

Our playing sites were much different from what kids like my son Chuck have today. Since outdoor ice isn't available much of the year in places like the Philadelphia area, most kids in the States must play indoors.

Our rinks were outdoors, usually in parks or school playgrounds. Drive through Philadelphia or New York and all you see are basketball courts near schools. Well, the hockey rinks were our answer to the basketball courts. Most rinks were lighted so we could practice at night. On many winter days I'd come home from school, get my equipment, and go to the rink for practice. I'd come home for dinner, then get some friends and go back to the rink. And our parents weren't able to drive us. It was either walk or take a bus. I probably should have been home studying. I know my parents wanted me to hit the books, but when they saw how much I loved hockey, I think they understood and were happy to see me interested in something.

There were times I wished I was carrying a heater in my equipment bag. As a Canadian, you get used to cold winters. But often when we were practicing in late afternoon or evening, the temperature would drop to 20° below zero. It was bone-chilling for the other players, too, but at least they could move around. I'd have to stand in front of the nets for minutes at a time. The goalie's equipment didn't help much in keeping me warm. Cripes, it's a miracle I didn't get frostbite.

The question I would get the most when the Flyers first started in Philly was "Why? Why do you play goal?" By that time it was a job, a job I felt capable of performing. But now, thinking back to those days when you were ten years old and freezing your butt off in the streets or an outdoor rink, you ask why you even did it. I wish I could come up with a revealing answer. Even then, there was pressure—to save the game for your team. The only answer must be I liked the challenge, even at eleven or twelve years old.

I would like to think the feeling is the same for pilots

and race-car drivers, that at an early age they realized they would *have* to fly or drive. I'm not that courageous; I used to hate flying and I'm not crazy about speed.

I loved playing shortstop in baseball, but a scout would have only rated me good field, fair hit. I was a little afraid of a pitched baseball. I never knew if I might be facing a hockey goalie who was getting revenge for guys shooting pucks at him.

One of my biggest thrills as a boy was at Christmas when I was about twelve. My parents gave me a set of goalie's pads that cost sixty-five dollars. Sixty-five dollars is a lot of money today, but in the mid-fifties it was a small fortune for our family.

When I opened the package on Christmas morning and saw the pads, my eyes must have been as bright as the Christmas tree lights. I was so excited I put the pads on over my pajamas, grabbed my goalie stick, and went out in the backyard. I stood in front of the net Yvan and Jacques had set up for me and pretended I was Plante making great saves against Gordie Howe and Alex Delvecchio in the Montreal-Detroit Stanley Cup finals. I wasn't imitating Plante too long, however, because I soon realized I forgot to put on skates or boots. Standing in the snow in your slippers is a good way to get pneumonia. Those pads must have been well made, because my son Chuck still wears them.

My mother came to almost all our games when I was playing for my brother's team, St. Victor's, in the midget leagues, and Rosemont in junior. She would bundle up and take the bus with other parents. My father didn't get to as many games as Mother. Maybe he was too busy working or too tired when he got home.

Remember, by the time I was a teen-ager Claude was in his fifties and had raised seven children.

My father is the one who introduced me to hunting. He liked to go hunting at Mt. Laurier, in northern Quebec. When I was about twelve years old, he would take me along, but I never got anything except a frozen butt.

If I recall correctly, I caught my first fish when I was about fourteen. The family was visiting my sister Raymonde and her husband, Jean-Aimé, in Howick, Quebec, about fifty miles from Montreal. After we talked for a while and the adults had some drinks (lemonade for me), I went fishing with Yvan in the Châteauguay River.

We had been fishing a couple hours when I felt a tug on my fishing line. I reeled in a nine-pound maskinonge, which is a fish in the pike family. I rushed back to Raymonde's house, thinking I was the world's greatest fisherman. Then a little while later, Yvan walked in holding a bigger fish. His maskinonge weighed thirteen pounds. I guess I caught the mother and Yvan caught the father. The family didn't hear much from the world's greatest fisherman the rest of the day.

By the time I was fourteen I was playing for St. Victor's. As they wrote in the French papers, I was *"gardien de buts du St. Victor."* I think I did a decent job. Roger Picard was the coach. It is people like Picard, Lionel Vinet, who coached St. Victor's my second year, and Herve Lalonde and Jacques St. Jean, my coaches at Rosemont, who are so vital to hockey. They are the ones who keep youngsters interested in hockey and teach them the fundamentals. The Picards and St.

Jeans don't make the money or get the **head**lines, but if it weren't for them, a lot of pro hockey players would be working in the mines, driving cabs, or waiting on tables.

In my final season for St. Victor's while I was attending school at St. François d'Assise on Lafontaine Street, I led the league's goaltenders in average. The leading scorer in the league was Ron Buchanan, who later was one of the World Hockey Association's leading scorers for Cleveland. Ron's father, Ralph, coached his team. Our paths crossed briefly my second season in Philadelphia when the Flyers drafted Ron from Boston. The year before he was one of Oklahoma City's top scorers. He never played for the Flyers, though. After starting the season with the Quebec Aces in the American Hockey League, he was sold to the St. Louis Blues.

Much to my parents' dismay, I was so occupied with hockey that I wasn't doing well in school. I had to repeat grade seven.

Something else I repeated was hiding in the bushes to see Jacques Plante. When I think of it now, it sounds silly.

Plante's sister, Thérèse, lived next door to us. Whenever we heard he was coming to visit her, we would run across the street and crouch down behind the bushes. Somehow I can't imagine kids today being as shy. Some kids today would wait on the sidewalk for Plante, open the car door for him, then ask for his autograph.

Our "secret meetings" with Plante were during the time when the Canadiens were hockey's super team. Starting with the 1955–56 season, the Canadiens won five consecutive Stanley Cups, which still stands as a record. Besides Plante, the Canadiens had great players such as Bernie Geoffrion, Jean Béliveau, Doug Harvey, Maurice (Rocket) Richard and his brother, Henri, Jean-Guy Talbot, Dickie Moore, and Tom Johnson.

Naturally, kids in Montreal idolized Plante and the Canadiens. We would listen to all the games on the radio and follow their games in the newspapers. During practice, I'd pretend I was Plante, and kids like Roger Vinet, our leading scorer for St. Victor's, would pretend they were the Rocket. If I would stop his shot, I'd holler, "Ah-ha, better go back to the minors, Rocket. Parent is too tough for you."

Playing in the National Hockey League and the winning of the two Stanley Cups with the Philadelphia Flyers are a long way from the days and nights practicing at the outdoor rinks. But I'll never forget the growing-up days in Montreal.

What's that book, *You Can't Go Home Again?* Maybe you can't, but you can remember, and sometimes remembering makes your days as a child the sweetest of all.

"BERNARD, YOU CAN'T PLAY HOCKEY ALL YOUR LIFE"

The first few months at Niagara Falls were certainly no honeymoon for me.

The world's first back-to-back Conn Smythe Trophy winner had a really impressive tryout with his first junior team.

While I was having a good year with St. Victor's, I was called up for a tryout with Rosemont, which was in the Montreal Metropolitan Junior League. Rosemont's goaltender had decided to enter the university and quit the team.

Playing for St. Victor's, I used to strap my pads on over my jeans. I never thought about that custom being foolish until I showed up for the Rosemont practice.

As I stepped onto the ice I could see people around the rink holding their hands over their faces and laughing. I never guessed that I looked silly.

After the workout, the Rosemont manager came over and said, "Thank you, I think we've found somebody else." I believed I had stopped some good shots, but being rejected didn't hit me that hard. I didn't really expect to make it at that time.

The following year Rosemont called me back and I made the club. Maybe they didn't have anybody else. With Rosemont we had the real McCoy—full uniforms, no more jeans on the ice. We also got paid.

Here I was, fifteen years old, and every Friday I got five dollars. Some kids these days get five-dollars allowance for doing nothing, but I was working my tail off. I didn't mind, of course. Playing hockey was all I cared about. I couldn't wait until high school classes at Chomedey de Maisonneuve were over so I could get to the rink.

The Montreal Metro League that Rosemont was in was high caliber, just a step below the Ontario Hockey Association (OHA). Only two players, Bob Berry of the Los Angeles Kings and Jacques Lemaire of Montreal, went on to the NHL besides me, but the Metro League was still good competition.

Until I got to Rosemont I had never worn a face mask. And my dental bill showed it. I had lost more than a few teeth on the ice. I quickly joined what was then a relatively new group of mask-wearers after getting hit over the right eye with a puck. It only took about nine stitches around the eye to close the cut. In the twenty or so years I've been a goaltender, that's the only time I've ever been cut on the face. Quick, let me touch wood!

During my first year with Rosemont, I got to see my first game at the Montreal Forum. Armand Mondou, who owned the Rosemont team, was a former Canadiens' player, and he got us tickets to see Chicago play. Plante was in the nets for Montreal, Glenn Hall played for Chicago. The game ended 1–1, and I went home walking three feet above the snowdrifts on Ste.-Catherine Street. I had just seen two of hockey's all-time great goalies play. Never at any time did I suspect that a few years later I would be on the same team with them for an NHL All-Star Game.

In my final year (1962–63) with Rosemont I got a raise—to five dollars a game—and we beat the Verdun Maple Leafs for the Metro Title. Bob Berry was one of Verdun's top players.

The way we beat Verdun was something I'll always remember. They won the first three games of the best-of-seven series, then we came back to win the next four.

Sounds familiar, eh? The New York Islanders came back from an 0–3 deficit to beat Pittsburgh in a 1975 Stanley Cup quarter-final series. Then the Islanders almost did the same thing to us.

After we beat Verdun, 3–0, to avoid elimination in the finals, the headline in the Montreal *Gazette* of March 25, 1963, read: PARENT KEEPS BOMBERS' HOPES ALIVE.

Part of the story by Bill Bennett read:

> Parent was particularly larcenous on Verdun's good left winger, Bob Berry. Parent frustrated Berry on two close-in power play thrusts in the second period. . . . Parent also closed the door on Verdun's All-Star defenseman Michel Hetu, who constantly had him hopping with booming drives from the blue line. Hetu was the hero of the second game of the series when one of his long shots eluded Parent for the game-winner.

Gerard Morin, our leading scorer, was the hero in the final game. We had come from behind to tie three times in the game, keeping the six thousand fans screaming. Then Morin scored early in overtime and we were the champs. We were all smiling and yelling as Jean-Guy Giroux, our captain, accepted the championship trophy.

I was named to the Metro League All-Star first team and led the league's goalies in average. Although it wasn't until I got to Niagara Falls in the OHA the following year that I seriously considered making the NHL, during the final season with Rosemont I began to think I might have what it takes.

I had developed a stand-up style that most NHL teams like. My timing was good, I challenged the shooters, and I loved to play. Still my parents and teachers had kept after me to get my education in case I got hurt and couldn't play hockey.

"Bernard," mother would say, "make sure you have a profession. You can't play hockey all your life and you may not make the NHL."

Emilie never pushed the education subject too much, though. Since she came to most games, maybe she had heard that scouts rated me an NHL prospect. And she knew how happy I was playing hockey. But, just to keep her happy, I said I'd like to be a coach and physical education teacher. After what I've seen coaches go through in the years since Rosemont, you couldn't get me near a coaching job even by offering me all the fish in the ocean.

From what I was told, my only problem as a goalie was stamina. Friends would tell me: "You have the talent, but you're not strong enough."

In our championship series against Verdun, I must have lost 20 to 25 pounds. At the time I only weighed 150 so I knew I'd have to build myself up.

Despite my lack of stamina, Boston must have liked something about me. Roland Mercier was a scout for the Bruins, and he recommended they draft Gilles Marotte and me.

After I was picked by Philadelphia in the expansion draft, hockey fans in Philly wondered how I wound up with Boston. I remember Joe Farruggio, a Flyers' fan who is a policeman in Ventnor, New Jersey, saying he thought the Montreal Canadiens had first claim on all French-Canadian junior players in Quebec.

Well, Rosemont was one of the few Montreal-area junior teams not sponsored by the Canadiens. As a kid I dreamed of playing for Montreal in the NHL, but as I got older it didn't matter that much. All that counted was playing in the NHL. Since Boston had finished last in the NHL in 1962–63, it had first choice of Quebec players. On Mercier's recommendation the Bruins took Marotte and me and assigned us to the Niagara Falls Flyers.

Leaving home for the first time wasn't easy. Emilie especially hated to see me go. I was the youngest and she knew this was it. If I continued on in hockey, I would never be home again except for visits.

After playing in Boston and Philadelphia, I learned that people in the States are amazed that Canadian boys sixteen and seventeen years old leave home to play hockey and can be traded. Most young men in the States who go on to college don't leave until they are eighteen or nineteen. Many parents in the States think sixteen is much too young to pack your skates and say goodbye to Mom and Dad.

Canadians don't think that way because we've been raised with the idea that if hockey is what you want and you're good enough, then you'll probably be moving hundreds of miles to play. What some people forget is that now, in most cases, the players must also finish high school.

Insisting the players get their diplomas is a big improvement over the previous system where many players would quit school in seventh or eighth grade at the club's insistence and concentrate on hockey. The trouble with that system was that when their playing careers were over, they had nothing to fall back on. Very few old-timers were as fortunate as a handful of today's, including me, whose contracts will protect them financially when they're finished playing.

Emilie and Claude took me to the train station in

downtown Montreal where I met Gilles Marotte. On the train ride to Niagara Falls my stomach was doing flip-flops. As I looked out the window and watched the train speed past the fields and houses, I tried to think of what Niagara Falls would be like.

I was concerned about how I would play, but I really wasn't too worried. If I concentrated, I felt I would do well because I had confidence and I knew we would have a good team.

My biggest worry on the train was the language. I hardly knew any English. We spoke only French around home and in the neighborhood. Marotte knew a little English, and he said he would help me, but, cripes, I couldn't be with Gilles every minute of the day.

As we approached Niagara Falls the conductor announced the station and I kept thinking, "Cripes, all I can say is *'Oui, oui,'* It's gonna be tough."

When we got off the train we saw Harold Cotton, who was a scout for Boston. I'll never forget, he had two gold teeth on the left side and a big cigar sticking out of his mouth. He said, "So you're Parent." Then he starts talking to us and I can't understand a damn thing he's saying. I almost got back on the train right then.

Somehow I resisted the temptation to turn around and go home. Gilles and I took a cab to the Niagara Falls rink, where we had to report. That's when we met Hap Emms for the first time. Emms, who later became manager of the Boston Bruins, was Niagara Falls owner. Bill Long was the coach.

Emms, whose real first name is Leighton, had a reputation for being tough. I found out he lived up to his reputation, but he was good for kids who wanted to learn and improve.

The discipline I have playing the game is due to him. At the time, you'd get mad as hell at him, but looking back, he helped a lot of us. He sent more players into pro hockey than any other coach. Just look at the guys on our team my first year there:

Marotte, Derek Sanderson, Doug Favell, Bill Goldsworthy, Ron Schock, John Arbour, Dave Woodley, Brian Bradley, and Ted Snell have all played in the NHL or WHA.

Emms was tough on and off the ice. For some reason, he wouldn't let us eat hot dogs or ice cream or play pool. For instance, when we'd travel from Niagara Falls to Peterborough, we'd stop near Toronto, which was about halfway. We'd have minute steaks, but Emms would say, "No ice cream." Maybe he thought it wasn't good for us. We knew the old man was watching his expenses, so maybe he was just being tight.

Playing for Niagara Falls was a step up the ladder in class and money. We got about fifty dollars a week that first year. Fifty dollars sounds pretty good until you remember that thirty dollars of it went for room and board and five dollars went for taxes. So we had fifteen left for assorted expenses like clothes—and girls. On that kind of money, a big night would be a movie and ice-cream sodas.

A good example of how tough Emms could be was the day he wanted to fine Marotte and me a hundred dollars apiece.

An Italian family in Niagara Falls had invited Marotte and me over for dinner. Cripes, they had everything —spaghetti, lasagna, salad. But there was no milk. We used to drink a lot of milk, and since we had just come from a tough practice I was dying of thirst.

"Angelo," the father said to the son, "go downstairs and bring up the wine."

We were eighteen and weren't supposed to drink, but we downed a couple jugs of red wine and got stiff. Gilles and I made a lot of noise and broke some things when we got back to our rooming house. We also got sick, so the landlady reported us to Emms.

Emms called us into his office before practice.

"So you guys got drunk last night," he said. "Well, I'm thinking of sending you home."

We started to panic. Looking at Gilles I could tell he was frightened. So was I. Cripes, neither of us wanted to go home. We were just eighteen-year-old kids who wanted to play hockey.

"Tell you what I'll do," Emms said after letting us work up a sweat. "Since your landlady said you were drinking in a private home and not in a bar, I'll fine you each one hundred dollars. Either the fine or you go home."

The old man knew what he was doing. He knew we didn't want to go home and be embarrassed. So we said we'd take the fine. Cripes, here we were being grateful to a guy who was taking a hundred dollars —two-weeks salary—away from us.

I'll say this for Emms, though: At the end of the season he gave the money back to us.

Emms is the one who helped me to play angles better. Until I turned eighteen I didn't know what a goaltender was supposed to do. I just did things by instinct. I was doing things, but I didn't know why.

One time Emms said, "You're not playing the angles right." I went home and said to myself, "What the hell does he mean by angles?" I really thought about it. With

Emms showing me how to cut down the room the shooter has, I began to realize what I was supposed to do.

The first few months at Niagara Falls were certainly no honeymoon for me. I got homesick, like I knew I would. The guys would go out after games, but I'd never go with them. I'd go back to my room and listen to Mitch Miller records. Those songs such as "Melancholy Baby" and "In My Solitude" would almost make me cry. Geez, I really felt lonely with the language barrier and being away from home.

It was during the first year at the Falls that I started appreciating my parents more. I started realizing how much they had done for me. Things such as my mother making my clothes, taking care of me, and coming to all the games, even though she didn't feel well.

When my mother died in 1973 while I was having money trouble with the Philadelphia Blazers, it hit me very hard. She had taken ill on a trip to Europe with Claude a few years before she died. From then on she was in and out of hospitals, so we knew it was only a matter of time.

Even though you know something like your mother dying is inevitable, when it happens, it still jolts you. I didn't show much emotion when I got the news, but inside I was upset. I thought back to things I wanted to say to Emilie, but never did. I just hoped she realized how much I loved her.

Since Emilie died, Claude and I have been closer than ever. My sister Louise, her husband, Jean Lortie, and their family live with Claude in the house on Bruxelles Street.

I call Claude once a week. He follows the team on

the radio, listening to Gene Hart and Don Earle or Ralph Lawler do the WCAU broadcasts. When we lose, Claude gives me hell.

"What are you doing?" he'll say. "You must be slipping."

Claude visits us in Wildwood in the summers and enjoys fishing and watching baseball games on television. He's still in great shape. He isn't a big man, but he is slender and very spry for seventy-two. I'd say he looks more like fifty-two than seventy-two.

That first season in Niagara Falls, which began for me with a 2–0 win over Kitchener, wasn't a success story as far as improving my English was concerned. After a while I was able to speak enough English to get by, but I remember once early in the season Marotte and I were at a restaurant in town called the Peacock. As we started walking back to our rooms, I said to Gilles (in French), "We got to start speaking in English."

"Okay," he said, "we'll speak English until we get to the house."

For the rest of the walk there wasn't one word spoken.

The first season in the Falls was good for me, as I was voted to the second OHA All-Star team. Chuck Goddard of Peterborough beat me for the first team by one vote. Sharing the goaltending with Doug Favell, I was among the OHA leaders in goals-against-average.

To emphasize how strong the OHA was, at one time that season, its leading scorers, in order, were: André Boudrias, Yvan Cournoyer, Fred Stanfield, Pete Stemkowski, Dennis Hull, Ron Ellis, and Ron Buchanan. Other top players in the league included Bobby Orr,

Doug Jarrett, Rod Seiling, Ken Hodge, Serge Savard, and Mike Walton. The goaltenders included Gary Smith and Rogie Vachon.

At the end of the play-offs, Marotte, Schock, and I were flown to Minneapolis where I served as a standby goalie for the Bruins' Central League farm club. I never played, but it was exciting experience seeing some pro action.

The following season Niagara Falls had an even better team. Added to the club were Jean Pronovost, Don Marcotte, and Rosey Paiement. Others in the league that year were André Lacroix, who would be my teammate and friend in Philadelphia, Danny Grant, and Mike Corrigan. Among the goalies were Dunc Wilson, Fern Rivard, Gerry Desjardins, and Peter McDuffe.

At that time, the Montreal Junior Canadiens were in the OHA, which meant I had the opportunity to play in the Forum. It was never filled as it is for Canadiens' games, but I thought playing there was something special. After one victory in the Forum, Doug Austin, sports editor of the Niagara Falls *Evening Review,* wrote:

> In recording his second shutout of this campaign, the handsome [no wonder I liked the story], round-faced youngster whose favorite player is Jacques Plante and who lives almost in the shadows of the Forum during the off-season, was magnificent for the quality of his saves, if not the quantity.

Montreal had "only" twenty-nine shots that night, which isn't too many for a junior game.

We finished first that season and won the play-offs. The fans voted me the team's most valuable player award. I had a 2.51 average, lowest in the league, while

Doug Favell had a 3.66 average in twenty-two games. Jean Pronovost was our leading scorer with 30 goals, 41 assists, and 71 points in fifty-five regular season games. Derek Sanderson was runner-up to Pronovost with 19-45-64 in fifty-five games.

Our series with Edmonton for the 1965 Memorial Cup, the junior championship of Canada, was a wild affair. We had to play in Edmonton, and early in the series a helluva brawl broke out. Ricky Ley of our club and Ron Anderson of the Oil Kings got into a stick-swinging duel. While they were fighting, Sanderson sucker-punched the bigger Bob Falkenberg. I didn't really get to know Sanderson, who was nicknamed the Turk, until we were teammates with the Philadelphia Blazers. Turk was from Niagara Falls, so we "visitors" didn't see much of him.

After the Turk hit Falkenberg, all hell broke loose. Fans were jumping on the ice trying to get at us. John Arbour grabbed my goalie stick and started swinging it at some fans. I was scared to death.

The brawl was finally broken up, but all the next day meetings were held at the MacDonald Hotel deciding whether to move the finals to Calgary. Hap Emms said, "This isn't hockey, it's war."

Through the Canadian Amateur Hockey Association (CAHA), maximum security was assured us. We went on to win the Memorial Cup. It's odd how things turn out. Edmonton's goalie was Wayne Stephenson, who is now my teammate in Philadelphia.

When we returned to Niagara Falls, we had a big parade. It was a great way to finish a junior career and a super send-off to Boston and the NHL.

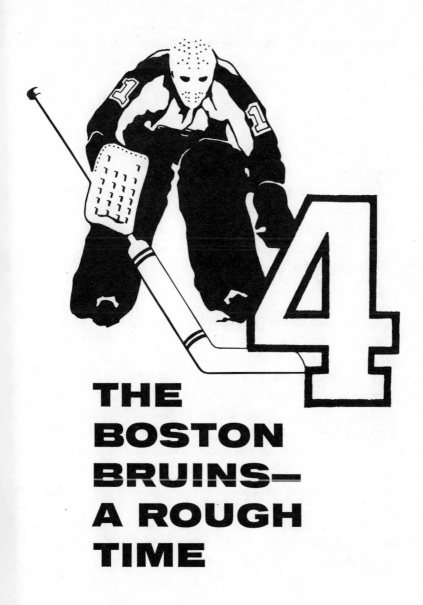

THE BOSTON BRUINS— A ROUGH TIME

I was playing so bad that the Boston fans were booing me. . . . throwing things at me, too.

My two-year stay with Boston got off to a great start.

The newspapers were calling me "the most sensational goalie in the business," and I was given credit for transforming the Bruins into a play-off contender. Both claims, of course, were exaggerated.

By play-off contender, incidentally, they meant fourth place. The Bruins had finished last for five years in a row and were far different from the Espositio-Orr-Cashman-Hodge-Bucyk club of recent years.

By the end of my second season in Boston, things weren't so good. Most of the problems were my own fault.

I reported to the Bruins' training camp in London, Ontario, in the fall of 1965. London is a nice university city southwest of Toronto on the way to Detroit.

I felt I had a good camp, but the Bruins had Eddie Johnston and Gerry Cheevers, so they sent Favvy and me down to Oklahoma City in the Central League. Some people probably thought I was acting like a wise rookie, because when the Bruins told me I was going to Oke City, I was pretty upset. Maybe I didn't know any better, but I thought I was at least ready for a shot at the NHL.

I knew it was almost impossible for a goalie to go right from junior to the NHL, especially in those days with only six NHL teams. Cheevers was also a rookie, but he had a couple years of minor league experience, so I guess the Bruins figured he deserved first chance.

Another thing was, I knew in those days a lot of good young goalies got buried in the minor leagues, and I

58

didn't want to be one of them. It was kind of scary thinking of it: NHL teams only needed two goalies apiece, so of all the goalies in hockey twelve lived like major leaguers and the rest rode buses.

The players liked Oke City, but I hardly had time to get fitted for a Western hat and cowboy boots. Johnston and Cheevers were injured early in the season and I was called up. Cripes, was I excited! I phoned home to tell my parents I was going up to Boston. Mother answered and was shocked when I broke her the news.

"Claude, Claude, it's Bernie, pick up the phone," she exclaimed.

When I told my father, he didn't seem as excited as my mother. All he said was "Show them you can do it, son."

The club was on the road in Chicago. I shared the warm-up with Jack Norris, the other goalie Boston called up from the Western League. I wasn't too nervous because I didn't think I'd play. Norris had played with the Bruins the year before.

Still, it was a thrill just being in Chicago Stadium. I tried to act cool, like an old pro just doing his job, but I was excited. Here I was on the same ice with guys like Glenn Hall, Pierre Pilote, Stan Mikita, and Bobby Hull. Mikita had won the NHL scoring title the year before, and Hull was headed for a fifty-four-goal season and the Hart Trophy.

When we returned to the dressing room, which in Chicago Stadium is down a flight of stairs, Milt Schmidt, who was coaching the Bruins, came over and said, "You're playing." I don't know what I said, probably something brilliant like "Okay, thanks." I was shocked. My first reaction was "Oh, my God!" It was a good thing we were going on the ice in a few minutes so I didn't have much time to think. Here I was, twenty years old, and playing in the NHL.

Don't ask much about the games because I don't remember the goals. All I know is we tied, 2–2. Guys like Ted Green, Murray Oliver, and Leo Boivin came around congratulating me, saying things like "Good start, kid." All I wanted to do was sit down. Whoever said the first NHL game in the nets is the hardest was right.

I don't know how much I had to do with it, but the team started playing well. We were 3–2–3 in my first eight starts. Two of the wins were over Montreal, which was in first place.

Beating the Canadiens in Montreal was another thrill. Geez, I was playing at the Forum against my hometown team with such players as Jean Béliveau, Henri Richard, Gilles Tremblay, and Jean-Guy Talbot. Bobby Rousseau scored first for Montreal, but Ron Stewart, Dean Prentice, and Ted Green scored for us, and we won, 3–1.

Montreal writers such as Jacques Beauchamps and Guy Emond, who had known me for a long time, were in the dressing room. They seemed happy for me. The win was also a good story for them: local boy makes good in home debut.

My first NHL shutout was against Toronto. Forbes Kennedy and Al Langlois scored. Johnny Bower was in the nets for the Maple Leafs. Somebody reminded me that Bower had played his first professional hockey game in 1945, the year I was born. Sorry, Pop.

Milt Schmidt said some nice things about me in the papers after the Toronto win.

"Parent has given this club the lift it needs," Schmidt

said. "He has all the moves, he stays up, and he stays remarkably cool."

Schmidt also said my only weakness was not knowing the opposition well. "But he's getting every opportunity to correct that," Schmidt added. I had no complaints: I was the one who wanted to play in the NHL.

Toward the end of the season we were playing in Chicago. I pulled a muscle with about one minute to play and Chicago winning. Cheevers had to go in and he wasn't pleased with the idea. He wasn't in top playing shape.

As Cheevers skated toward the net, he told our defensemen, "Don't let Bobby Hull get a shot."

A couple seconds later, Stan Mikita passed the puck to Hull, and he let one go about ninety miles an hour right past Cheevers's head for a goal. Cheevers never saw the bleeping puck. Later, in the dressing room, he was still in shock.

I played in thirty-nine games that season and wound up with a 3.69 average. Not too bad for a losing team. The Bruins had a 21–43–6 record, but finally climbed out of last place—one point ahead of the Rangers.

Generally it was a decent first season, but things were happening that would make the next year, my last in Boston, miserable.

The first month after I was called up to Boston I lived in the Madison Hotel, which is next to Boston Garden. The Madison is an old place where the NHL game officials used to stay because it's so convenient.

The rest of the season I lived in North Quincy, Massachusetts, with Bill Callahan. His son had been a stick boy with the Bruins.

Mr. Callahan used to follow hockey, but then his wife died and he lost interest. While I was staying with him, I talked him into coming out to watch some games. He got interested again, and now he even visits Claude in Montreal in the summers.

Mr. Callahan used to cook for me. I hope he won't feel bad, but I'm lucky I didn't starve.

On the road I roomed with Eddie Johnston. He was about thirty then and had been Boston's regular goalie, so he was a big help filling me in on players in the league.

Playing with Boston was a tough experience because I was a kid on a team with mainly older people. We had a couple of young guys like Don Awrey and Ron Schock, my teammate at Niagara Falls, but it was mostly a veteran team and I was too young to handle the pressure.

There were a lot of temptations around Boston then for a young hockey player. You're twenty years old and making pretty good money. It's not an easy situation to handle.

I didn't know how to pick my spots to have fun. There's nothing wrong with partying, but not the night before a game. If you're playing Thursday night, it's okay to have a few drinks Monday or Tuesday, but you should lay off before the game. It's hard to say no if people you know are partying, but if you think you have talent and want to play in the major leagues, the time to start taking care of yourself is in your younger years. I was never hung-over for a game, but there were times I was tired and couldn't produce.

Harry Sinden took over as coach my second season in Boston, with Milt Schmidt moving up to general manager. Sinden was an energetic young guy who had coached the Bruins' system in Minneapolis and Oklahoma City.

Sinden came to Boston at the right time because his first year was Bobby Orr's rookie year. Orr had had a big publicity buildup before he signed. Naturally, we wondered how good he really was. Well, he was everything they said—and more. When Bobby first came up, he was just eighteen years old and wasn't bothered by the bad knees he has now. If you think he can skate now, you should have seen him fly then. Cripes, nobody could keep up with him.

Bobby won the Calder Trophy as rookie of the year for the 1966–67 season. You could win trivia contests by naming the runner-up to Orr in the voting. It was Ed Van Impe, our defenseman in Philly, who was then with Chicago.

Unfortunately, I didn't get a chance to know Sinden well. The club got off to a bad start and I was playing lousy. One time Johnston got a skate cut on his forehead and had to leave the game. Sinden turned to me on the bench and said, "Well, I guess you have to go in."

Great, eh? It sounded like he wished he had somebody else to use. Ah, the way I was going I probably wished Sinden had somebody else, too.

I was playing so bad that the Boston fans were booing me. They were throwing things at me, too. Quite a change from the year before, but I couldn't blame them. The club was always out of the play-off picture by Christmas. Maybe we had built up their hopes the year before. Now we were letting them down.

If an athlete ever tells you booing doesn't bother

him, he's either in a trance or just plain ignorant. Maybe in a big football or baseball stadium or in an arena like Madison Square Garden where the fans aren't right on top of the players you don't notice the fans' reaction as much. But in places such as Boston Garden and the Spectrum, where the fans are close to the ice, a player has to hear the boos.

The way the Boston fans were booing me, I'd go home and ask myself, "What's a nice guy like you doing in a place like this?" I'd ask myself what I was doing wrong. I wanted to play well and produce.

Of course, my first move should have been to take better care of myself. But like I said, when you're young and making good money, it's hard to resist the good times.

The fans getting on me took all the enjoyment out of playing the game. Comparing what we've accomplished in Philadelphia to what it was like in Boston is like the difference between catching a marlin and falling overboard. Catch a marlin and you feel like a million bucks. Fall overboard and you feel like a fool. In Boston I was scared of going on the ice, making mistakes and looking like a fool.

Schmidt and Sinden must have seen what was happening because I finished the season in Oklahoma City. My average was 3.64 in Boston. Going to the minors was probably the best thing for the club and me. Favvy had been in Oke City all season and had a good average, 2.62. In fourteen games there my average was 2.70 with four shutouts. I felt like I had gotten my game together again, even if it was in the minor leagues.

I don't think many Boston fans were sorry to see me

I look very well behaved, maybe I was too young to get into any kind of trouble. That all came later.

As a six year old — again a model of decorum.

1951

Here I am opening up a Christmas present from my mom and dad at age seven —my very first pair of skates. It feels good to remember that day.

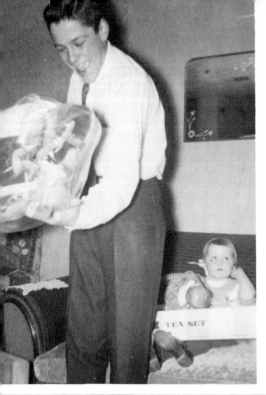

Another first—goalie's pads from Mom and Dad. I'm fifteen years old.

A family celebration marking my parents thirtieth wedding anniversary. First row: my father, me, my mother and sister Thérèse. Second row: Louise, Jacques, Raymonde, Yvan, Marie-Claude.

A young hockey player — about age seventeen.

Our championship Rosemount team from the Montreal Metro League. It's easy to pick me out — I guess I haven't changed that much.

I was elected the Most Valuable Player on the 1964-65 Niagara Falls Flyers. The two previous years Terry Crisp and Ron Schock had won so I was in good company.

Ed Snider tries to console me after my trade to Toronto. I remember how bad I felt and this picture brings it all back.

I have just made a tough save against Dennis Hull who has just about as hard a shot as anyone around. Moose Dupont looks worried.

Against the oncoming Rod Gilbert I drop on the puck. Bill Barber follows the play and Bobby Clarke practices pull-ups on the goal. Actually, Bobby's hustling back on defense resulted in this slide into the goal.

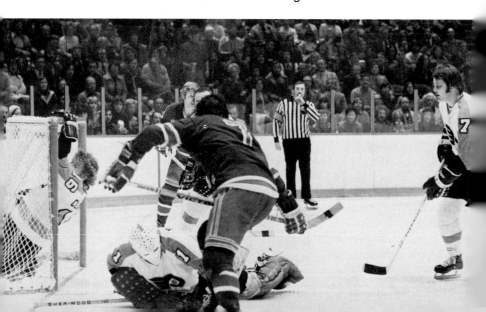

go. After finishing fifth my rookie year, the club dropped anchor again in last place, fourteen points behind Detroit.

By the end of the season we all knew the NHL's first expansion draft would be held in June. I wasn't sure how it would affect me.

Cheevers finished the season in Boston with a 3.33 average. He was about four years older than I, so I guess the Bruins figured he was more mature and better prepared to handle the pressure of an NHL goaltender.

The Bruins protected Cheevers and Johnston, so Philadelphia drafted me as its first pick. The only surprise was I thought Boston might leave Johnston unprotected. I thought Philadelphia would take an experienced goalie like E.J., but I guess they wanted to start with young goalies because they also picked Favell.

Philadelphia almost didn't have a chance to pick me. A few weeks before the expansion draft the Bruins and Black Hawks made that big deal with Phil Esposito, Ken Hodge, and Fred Stanfield going to Boston for Gilles Marotte, Pit Martin, and Jack Norris. I have heard that Boston told the Black Hawks they would get a young goalie in the deal. Tommy Ivan, Chicago's general manager, thought the young goalie would be me, but instead it was Norris.

Ivan didn't give up because after the deal was completed, there were stories that he was offering Philadelphia $250,000 for me. Geez, the Black Hawks didn't get Tony Esposito until two years later. A Parent-Esposito combination in goal for Chicago would have been tough, eh?

73

In a way, I felt bad about leaving Boston. I had let the club down by not looking after myself more.

If I knew then how playing in Philadelphia would turn out for me, I would have hired the nearest boat and crossed the Delaware River just like George Washington did (in the opposite direction, of course). But when you're twenty-two and traded for the first time, you don't know what to think. It's your first move, so it's kind of a shock, but you accept it.

I did get some good advice after Philadelphia picked me. Somebody told me I'd better smarten up, that I wouldn't get many more chances like going to Philadelphia.

I'm glad I took the advice.

5

THE START OF A LOVE AFFAIR— THE FLYERS IN 1967

Now I was part of the best goaltending team in the league.

When the Flyers opened their first NHL season in 1967, I'm sure most of us were strangers to Philadelphia fans. Hell, most of the people coming to the Spectrum, which had to be built for Philadelphia to obtain an NHL franchise, were strangers to hockey.

Philadelphia had had some minor league hockey teams, but now they had the real McCoy: the NHL, with Bobby Hull, Gordie Howe, Jean Béliveau, Bobby Orr, Phil Esposito, Glenn Hall, Jacques Plante—and us.

The NHL was smart in handling expansion. The six new teams—St. Louis, Minnesota, Pittsburgh, Oakland, Los Angeles, and us—were put in one division, and we played each other twice as often as we played the established teams. The result was just what the league dreamed of: In the final division standings only six points separated the first five teams.

The best thing we did for hockey in Philadelphia that first season was finish in first place. Even though we had a losing record (31-32-11) and were only one point ahead of L.A., we had won a title. Philly fans who didn't know much about the game must have figured, "Hey, these guys might have something going for them."

Those first-year Flyers weren't a real colorful team like our Stanley Cup champions. Geez, our highest scorer, Lou Angotti, had only forty-nine points (Stan Mikita led the NHL in scoring that year with eighty-seven points.)

Players drafted by the Flyers were either young such as Dougie, Joe Watson, Brit Selby (the 1966 Calder Trophy winner), and myself; older guys with limited

NHL experience such as Eddie Van Impe and Leon Rochefort; or players such as Jimmy Johnson, Don Blackburn, Gary Dornhoefer, and Pat Hannigan, who had good minor-league records but hadn't had a chance to crack an NHL lineup.

The Flyers' front office also made a good move before the expansion draft by buying the Quebec Aces of the American League. Players who moved up to the Flyers from Quebec included Bill Sutherland, Ed Hoekstra, and our "French Line" of André Lacroix, Jean-Guy Gendron, and Simon Nolet.

Bud Poile, who was the Flyers' general manager, and Keith Allen, the club's first coach who is now G.M., didn't try hiding they were stressing defense. They were counting on Dougie and me to keep the scores down. Winning 2–1 or 3–2 is just as good as winning 8–1, although not as much fun. Nearly all the expansion teams were also thinking defense as their draft of experienced goalies shows: the late Terry Sawchuk by L.A., Glenn Hall by St. Louis, and Charlie Hodge by Oakland.

Sutherland, who was our only twenty-goal scorer except for "Cheesy" Rochefort, had an unforgettable introduction to the Spectrum. We were so new to the city that even people at the Spectrum didn't know all of us. "Suds" didn't have his pass, so the ushers wouldn't let him in on opening night. He had to sneak into the building. We were glad he did, because he scored the only goal as we beat Pittsburgh 1–0 before over seven thousand fans.

We kept playing well and were in first place by Christmas. One of our biggest wins was over Montreal—at the Forum! The Canadiens outshot us

39–14, but we won 4–1 with Rochefort scoring the hat trick. Two of Philly's Frenchmen had struck back!

Beating the Canadiens meant a lot to us because I was from Montreal and "Cheesy" had been drafted by Philadelphia from the Canadiens. You always like beating the team that let you go. Regardless of how they try to butter you up, when you're traded, they didn't think you could help them enough or you would have stayed.

The mid-season point of that first year in Philly was important to Favvy and me because we were leading the Vezina Trophy race. Our combined average was just a little over 2.00. The award money was only $250, which we split. By today's standards, $125 would only buy an expensive box of cigars and a fancy dinner for the wife.

Money, of course, wasn't what counted. The year before, I had been booed out of Boston and wound up in the minor leagues. Now I was part of the best goaltending team in the NHL.

Finishing first wasn't easy because for the last month we were always on the road. The reason was the Spectrum roof blew off. Well, it wasn't the entire roof. During an ice show in February the wind tore some pieces off the roof. Repairs were made, but the roof was damaged again and the city had to close the building. The Spectrum was reopened for our play-offs, but in the meantime we became real vagabonds, playing "home" games in Toronto, New York, and Quebec City.

In a game at Toronto against Boston, Larry Zeidel, one of our defensemen, got into a terrible stick fight with Eddie Shack. Zeidel, whose nickname was Rock, had had trouble with the Bruins before. Rock said the Bruins had been making remarks about him being Jewish. A stick fight is a frightening thing to see and even worse to be involved in. Just look what happened in the Ted Green–Wayne Maki stick fight: Green suffered head injuries and Maki was hounded by the Bruins. Maki died a couple years ago from a brain tumor.

Another "home" game I remember is a 0–0 tie with Los Angeles in Quebec City. We had played in Minnesota, then flown to Quebec, arriving at six o'clock in the morning. We all went right to bed at the Château Frontenac. A couple hours later, I'm told, workmen started drilling near our rooms. Most of the guys were really ticked off, but not me. I didn't hear a thing.

On the final weekend of the season, we played in Quebec City, then flew to Pittsburgh. L.A. and Oakland were playing on the West Coast. When L.A. tied, we had clinched the division title and Mr. Snider threw a party. I'm afraid the Pittsburgh fans didn't get their money's worth the next night.

Our first play-off appearance had much to do with creating hockey interest in Philly. We already had a big rivalry going with St. Louis, on and off the ice. St. Louis had the Plager brothers, Barclay and Bob, and Noel Picard, a tough defenseman, and they used to push us around. In those early days, we were a long way from being the "Broad Street Bullies."

Off the ice, Bud Poile and Scotty Bowman, the Blues' G.M.-coach, had a strong dislike for each other. I'm not sure what caused it, but there were times they'd be shouting at each other in the corridors after games.

Poile had been a good defenseman in the NHL. Both he and Keith Allen had come to Philly from the Western League. Poile had been G.M.-coach at San Francisco while Keith had the same jobs with Seattle.

Bud, who is now an executive with the World Hockey Association, knew hockey talent, but he was so excitable and wanted to win so badly that sometimes he'd forget himself.

Once, while a game was under way, Bud was pacing the press box. We must not have been playing too well and he happened to walk by the St. Louis radio announcers, Dan Kelly and Gus Kyle. Kyle, who had played against Bud in the NHL, said something Bud didn't like because Bud started shouting at him. Kyle had a temper, too, so he hollered back—and the St. Louis listeners were treated to a lively, unrehearsed argument.

Another time, Bud was so upset by the team that he dashed out of the Spectrum after the game and drove to his suburban home in Bryn Mawr, Pennsylvania. The only problem was his wife, Margaret, was still in the Spectrum. It's a good thing Mrs. Poile had cab fare that night.

Things were lively on the ice, too. Our play-off series with St. Louis was rough, with Clarence Campbell fining both teams a total of $3,800 after one brawl. There was also some good hockey played.

In fact, one game in the series is the one I consider the best I've ever played in the NHL, including our two Stanley Cup seasons.

Any time a goalie makes sixty-three saves, it's a big game, right? What made the game more meaningful was we needed a win to stay alive in the play-offs.

St. Louis was leading, 1–0, when Andy Lacroix scored against Glenn Hall with only fifteen seconds left in regulation. We were playing in St. Louis Arena, and the crowd was already standing and cheering the

Blues when Andy scored. To be honest, I didn't think we had a chance to tie or win it.

The game went into the second overtime with Blackburn finally winning it for us at 11:18 on a fifty-foot shot that he just lobbed at Hall. Blackie said he wasn't even trying to shoot. In the dressing room my hand was shaking so much from fatigue that I couldn't drink a cup of water.

That win, tying the series at 3–3, should have given us a big lift, but we went back to Philly and, before a sellout crowd, lost 3–1. St. Louis brought Doug Harvey, the great NHL defenseman, who was coaching the Blues' farm team at Kansas City. Cripes, Harvey was about forty-three years old, but he controlled that seventh game the way Bobby Orr controls a game today. It was Harvey who fed Larry Keenan for the winning goal.

Even though we were knocked out of the play-offs, it had been a good season. The series with the Blues had hooked a lot of Philly fans on hockey, and we had every reason to think the next season would be better.

It wasn't.

We finished third, which might not be bad except we were twenty-seven points behind St. Louis and eight behind Oakland. We only beat out L.A. for third by three points. That was the season Red Berenson scored six goals in one game against Favvy and we lost, 8–0. Another time, we were smashed by Chicago, 12–0. Favvy and I shared that misery. What made those losses worse was both were at the Spectrum.

In the play-offs St. Louis wiped us out in four straight. It was after the humiliation that Mr. Snider told Poile to get some bigger players. So in the 1969 amateur draft, the Flyers picked Dave Schultz, Don Saleski, and Willie Brossart. The Flyers' top pick that year was Bobby Clarke, who in his own way is as tough a hockey player as there is.

There were some good spots that second season. In one weekend we beat Toronto in Maple Leaf Gardens and Montreal at the Spectrum. Both wins were by 3–2 and I was in goal. I played in the All-Star Game in Montreal. Hall, Plante, and I each played one period. In my twenty minutes the East didn't score and the game ended 3–3.

When we'd have a good weekend like we did against Toronto and Montreal, we liked to think we were improving. But the truth was any time we beat an older team it was usually a fluke. I don't think they meant to let down against the new teams, but it happened. I'm sure they had as much trouble getting up for us as we do now for Washington and Kansas City. This is no knock at those two teams, but we know that if we play our game, we should beat them.

The early Flyers had an inferiority complex when we faced teams like Montreal, Toronto, Chicago, and Boston. It wasn't a matter of winning—we just hoped to keep the score close. If we got good goaltending and everybody checked, then we had a chance to win. It was probably dull hockey, but it was either that or get chased out of the building.

To their credit, players on the older teams never made remarks putting us down. They never called us rejects or things like that. Most players have too much respect for others to cut them up.

Phil Esposito is about the only player I can remember saying anything during a game that ticked me off. Even times when I got mad and went after some-body, like Dave Balon with Minnesota, it was something he did, not said. In that case, I had smothered the puck, but he kept poking at it. I slashed at him with my stick, then ripped off my mask and went after him. Balon was probably as surprised as I was, but in the heat of the game you sometimes don't act like yourself.

Esposito's crack occurred the last time we played Boston during the regular season in 1974, the year Tony Esposito and I had the close race for the Vezina Trophy. Near the end of the game that we won to clinch the division championship, Phil skated by me and said:

"You'll never catch my brother."

At the time what Phil said hurt me because, what the hell, I'd never said anything about Tony. I thought Phil was acting bush, but then I realized he was just trying to psyche me out and I couldn't blame him.

During the first couple seasons nearly all the players were living in apartments in Barrington, New Jersey. It's about a ten-minute drive from Barrington to the Walt Whitman Bridge near the Spectrum. It's natural for players on a new team to live in the same area. You don't know many people outside hockey so it's nice for the wives and families of the players, especially when the team is on the road.

Bud Poile came up with a funny story the second season concerning wives and families. It was hard to tell if Bud was serious, but since all he thought about during the season was winning I guess he wasn't kid-ding.

We read in a Philadelphia *Evening Bulletin* story by John Brogan, who is now the Flyers' publicity director, that Bud said wives were distracting the players.

83

"The players have been worrying about getting their families settled," Bud said. "They haven't been thinking hockey twenty-four hours a day."

Bud didn't want the players bothered by washing dishes, baby-sitting, or changing diapers.

"The girls like the nice clothes that hockey buys and they like to go to Florida after the season," he said. "Well, they have to sacrifice if they want that."

I wasn't married yet, but I'll bet when the wives read that, they wanted to sacrifice Poile—in the nearest fire. He did have a point, though. On game days, a player can't be running around doing errands and working around the house. Our workday is reversed from that of most people. We're around home all day, then have to go to work—in front of thousands of people. We have to get our rest, or soon teams won't want us for "night work," or any other work.

At the end of the second season I signed a new three-year contract that started at $20,000 a year plus bonuses. That money sounds low compared to what many of us earn today, but then I was happy with it.

The third season in Philly was pretty dismal. On the ice, that is. That's the year Carol and I got married before the season, so I felt great.

There's a story from early in that season that shows what a good time we were having. We were living in Barrington and I was packing for a road trip on Halloween. Carol said she and her sister, Dot Smith, were going upstairs to visit a neighbor, Edna Lockwood.

I was still packing when I heard a knock at the door. Answering the door or telephone is not my favorite pastime. When I heard a knock, I ignored it awhile.

Finally, I answered the door and saw two people, one dressed as a hunter, the other as a clown.

"Trick or treat," they said, so I gave them some candy. They just stood there, so I said, "I have to go now."

Suddenly, they just pushed past me into the apartment.

When I asked if I knew them, the one dressed like a hunter, said no, then grabbed all the candy we had on the table. When I tried to take it away, the "hunter" grabbed for my waist.

"Hey, what are you doing?" I yelled.

I could hear the players outside beeping for me when Carol finally took off her hunter's mask. Geez, I had to admit they completely fooled me. Carol was even wearing my own hunting clothes.

On the ice, the team wasn't having as much fun. We were struggling. Clarkie was a rookie, and you could tell he would help us, but we were having trouble scoring goals. That's the year we set the NHL record for most ties, twenty-four, and missed the play-offs.

I blamed myself for us not making the play-offs. Minnesota knocked us out of a play-off spot by winning 1–0 on the last weekend of the season. Barry Gibbs scored a fluke goal to beat us.

It was an afternoon game at the Spectrum and Gibbs let the puck go from center ice. I don't think it was even a shot. But I never saw it.

If that double overtime win against St. Louis was the best game of my career, then Gibbs's goal was the worst goal I ever allowed.

6

"I'VE GOT SOME BAD NEWS"

Going to Toronto

Trades are a part of professional sports that can cause mixed emotions. Generally, trades mean two things: Somebody doesn't want you enough to keep you and somebody else wants you badly enough to break up their team to get you.

Most of the time it's tough watching a teammate pack his gear. He tries to keep smiling while he says his goodbyes around the dressing room. You walk up to him, shake hands, and tell him, "It's probably for the best."

Deep down inside, though, you know he's hurt. After he first hears he has been traded he doesn't even stop to think about where he's going or what guys he'll be playing with. He just figures his talent wasn't enough for his club to keep him. Hey, I know about trades. I've been down that road.

In early January 1971 trade rumors were flying around our locker room. Favvy and I took turns ribbing each other about where we'd be playing and what the club would get for us in return. Our club needed help offensively, and it was rumored that management was willing to trade to get it.

Ed Snider, Flyers' board chairman, was never impatient about winning like some expansion teams. But by the 1970–71 season I think he realized the Flyers weren't making really big strides toward challenging for the Stanley Cup. I think he, General Manager Keith Allen, and Marcel Pelletier, Keith's assistant, decided they had to take a gamble, make a big move toward improving the club.

By late January the trade talk wasn't a joking matter

anymore. We had definite reports a trade was in the works.

Maybe I should have sensed something would go wrong for me on the night of Sunday, January 31.

For the first time that season, Carol wasn't at the Spectrum for a game. She had been feeling lousy all day, but planned to make the game anyhow. It was a bitter cold night, so I suggested she stay home. She finally agreed and bundled herself up on the living room couch.

"I'll listen to the game on the radio," she said as I closed the door behind me.

We were playing Detroit, and Favvy was in goal. After the game, which we won 3-1, I was sitting at my locker loosening my pads when Vic Stasiuk, the coach, walked over.

"Keith wants to see you right away," Vic said. I nodded and said I'd be with Keith as soon as I showered and got dressed.

Vic's words bothered me. They had caught me completely off guard. I had never before been asked to see Keith after a game.

Right away, I had a bad feeling. Although my mind kept telling me, "This is it," I couldn't believe it. It's funny, when it comes right down to trades, you always think it's going to happen to the other guy. Never you. But this time I figured I was "the other guy."

I guess I delayed going to Keith's office as long as I could. I showered and kidded with the guys such as Joe Watson, Favvy, Eddie Van Impe, Guy Gendron, Andy Lacroix, and Jimmy Johnson. I even told Favvy, "Here I go." Inside, though, I was still hoping it wasn't really me who was leaving.

Carol and I did not want to leave Philadelphia.

She was from the Cherry Hill, New Jersey, area and had never been much farther from Philly than the seashore. Her whole family and all her friends lived in the area. And me, well, I had grown to love Philadelphia.

The club was young and headed in the right direction. Bobby Clarke was clearly a future superstar. His style of play and his enthusiasm were catching on with the entire team. And the Philly fans, supposedly very critical, were starting to appreciate major-league hockey. It seemed the days of being regarded as merely an expansion hockey team were nearly behind us. Philly seemed like the ideal place to stay and grow.

After dressing, I left the locker room and walked down the Spectrum corridor leading to the Flyers' offices. It's not a long walk, maybe a hundred feet, but now that I was away from the guys many thoughts entered my mind. The main thought was I kept praying it really wasn't my turn to go.

As I entered Keith's office he was standing behind his desk. My friend, Marcel Pelletier, was alongside him. I sat down and looked up at Keith.

"You've just been traded to Toronto," he said quickly.

I heard the words and opened my mouth to say something, but nothing came out. My mouth was dry as stale toast. I continued to look at Keith, but was so shocked I couldn't speak. It was a very uneasy moment.

"This is the hardest trade I've ever made," Keith said, breaking the silence. Then he gave me that old bull about "To get what we wanted we had to give you."

I was afraid I'd say something I'd regret, so I got up

and left without a word. When I reached the hallway, I bumped into Mr. Snider.

He must have noticed the tears in my eyes. I guess he felt lousy, too. He tried to make me feel better.

"Look, Bernie, I didn't want to do it," Snider said. "I feel bad about it, but it's part of the game. We have to progress."

I was so choked up, I still couldn't talk. I left the Spectrum all alone. Usually, some fans would be waiting outside for autographs. But not this cold winter night. Because of the late hour and below-freezing temperature, they had all gone.

Normally Carol would have been walking back to the car with me. But she was home. There was no one but me. I wondered whether my wife had heard the trade news on the radio. As I got into my car, I turned and took a long, hard look at the Spectrum. That's when it really hit me. I figured that this would be the last time I'd be seeing the Spectrum as a Flyer. Sure, I'd be back in that building again, but not with Philadelphia.

The Walt Whitman Bridge spans the Delaware River separating Jersey from Pennsylvania. It's a five-minute drive from the Spectrum to the bridge. Our new home in Cherry Hill was a twenty-minute ride from the bridge. Driving over the Walt Whitman, I kept glancing up at the sky. Although it was cold, it was a clear night and the stars were shining brightly. There was little traffic. As I drove I tried to straighten out my thoughts.

I was young and wasn't really mature yet. Cripes, I had never before been through anything as shocking as this. From the time you're a junior in hockey, you learn to adapt to different teams and different organizations. Like when I was with Niagara Falls in the OHA we had a strong two-way team. We scored a lot of goals, but played good, tough defense, too. I never worried about being traded because I had a pretty good (goals against) average and I knew the Bruins regarded me as a top prospect.

I had that same feeling with the Flyers. I figured I'd be around with them for a long time. Okay, so I was sharing the goaltending with Favell. Still, I knew Flyers' management thought highly of me. Marcel constantly told me the brass was satisfied with the way I was playing.

A couple years later I would remember that's the same crap they fed Andy Lacroix for a while. Andy had been with the Flyers' organization since it started. He even married a Philadelphia girl and was the first Flyer to go into business in Philly. He and Ed Van Impe opened a skating rink together.

Geez, Andy could handle the puck. In hockey, twenty goals is considered a good season, and Andy had three straight twenty-goal seasons for the Flyers. He was real popular with the Philly fans, but after a while his popularity or goal scoring didn't mean a thing to Vic. Stasiuk was from the old school. He liked his players big and tough. Andy stood only 5′ 8″ and weighed around 170. Vic probably thought Andy would have been better off sitting in a sulky racing trotters at Blue Bonnets in Montreal.

Despite Andy's talents and the fact that management had praised him early in his career with the Flyers, Vic played him so little that he was traded to Chicago early the next season for Rick Foley, a rugged, mean defenseman—and a man after Stasiuk's heart. As it turned out, when the Flyers got Foley, Vic had been replaced by Fred Shero.

But that couldn't save poor Andy. He had already been axed. Chicago wanted him because they needed someone to center for Bobby Hull. Still, Chicago wasn't the place for Andy either.

I know Andy could have done the job with the Flyers. But I believe his terrible disappointment in being traded from Philly, where his talents weren't appreciated, carried over all through that season with Chicago. Andy Lacroix had gone on to become one of the best scorers in the WHA, but I'm sure he'll never forget the way he was mistreated by Vic Stasiuk in Philadelphia.

Some of these same thoughts were racing through my mind as I got closer to home. Reaching my driveway, I kept trying to tell myself to look at it positively. The Flyers traded me because they wanted to improve themselves. They thought they could get something good for me. They got Mike Walton, a pretty decent young scorer; Bruce Gamble, a steady veteran goaltender; and Toronto's first-round draft choice in 1971, who turned out to be Pierre Plante, now a thirty-goal scorer for St. Louis. Walton never put on a Flyers' uniform because he was traded to Boston for Rick Mac-Leish and Danny Schock. Two years later, Ricky became a fifty-goal scorer for Philly and has been a key man on our Stanley Cup champions.

But at the time, I didn't even know what other players were involved in the trade. I had been so completely stunned when I heard the word from Keith that I never gave a damn about who the Flyers got for me.

Now my main concern was to break the bad news to my wife as gently as possible. I'd always believed that a man could be successful in business, yet still be a failure as a man. I had been successful in professional hockey, but was I a failure as a man? I was having my doubts. Here I had established myself in Philly. I thought I was successful in my profession, but was I failing my wife and family as a man?

We were living in our new Cherry Hill home. Everything was going along smoothly. Most of the Flyers were good guys. Then two general managers hundreds of miles apart spoke over the telephone and rearranged my whole life. One wanted me, the other didn't want me enough to keep me. Instead Keith Allen had used me as bait to get something he thought would help the club more than me. Yeah, maybe at twenty-five I was a failure as a man.

When I went in the house, Carol was still all bundled up on the couch. She was watching the eleven o'clock news on TV. I hung up my fur coat in the hallway closet. Had she gotten the word yet? Finally, I sort of tiptoed into the living room and said to myself, "Ah, hell, I may as well get it over with already."

"Hey, hon, I've got some bad news," I kind of whispered to her.

She sat up with a worried look on her face.

"What's the matter?" she wanted to know, obviously unaware of the trade.

"We're going to Toronto. . . ."

She took it real rough. Just the same as I had. At first she couldn't say a word. Then she started crying.

Seeing her tears got me going again. It was awful.

Here we were, like two little kids, bawling as if we had just found coal in our stockings on Christmas morning.

The only things Carol knew about Toronto was that it was a city in Canada and that it had a hockey team called the Maple Leafs.

I could see it was going to be hard for her to leave home.

Then I figured I had to do something to change the mood. I got a bottle of Cold Duck from the refrigerator, popped it open, and we both started drinking.

The Philadelphia hockey writers who had missed me at the Spectrum started calling. I had left before they were called into a press conference. I asked them to call me again Monday because I wanted to keep the lines open.

Earlier that night, Carol had taken a message from a long-distance operator saying that Jim Gregory from Toronto was trying to reach me and would call later. At that time, Carol didn't even know who Gregory was.

Around midnight, Gregory, Toronto's general manager, got through. He wanted to know if I was happy with the trade. What could I say? I told him I was upset at leaving Philly, but I said that no matter who I played for, I'd give it my best shot.

Gregory said Toronto had a home game that Wednesday night. They wanted me to report Tuesday. I told him I'd try, but I wasn't leaving without my family.

It's not easy moving in one day. Most business executives I know who are transferred are allowed at least a couple of weeks to get their personal things in order. Sports teams expect you to move faster.

Helping us pack were my hunting friend, Ray

Marella, and his wife, Joan, of Berlin, New Jersey, and Carol's friend Judy Rafter. Carol was busy canceling doctor's appointments, telephone service, the newspapers, and notifying the post office of our address change.

Somehow, by Tuesday morning we were ready. Ray and I had hitched a U-Haul trailer to his car. Then we packed everyone in our car: Chuck, who was seven; Bernie, Jr., who was nine months old; our dog, Tinker; and two gerbils.

What a trip that was. It was more like a nightmare.

Carol was changing Bernie Junior's diapers in the back of our '68 Chrysler and he kept howling. Around Syracuse, New York, it started to snow. Coming from Canada, I had seen some fierce snowstorms. But this one could have matched any of them. What a blizzard!

It got so bad the police closed down the highway. We pulled into the first hotel we saw. We just wanted to escape the kid's screaming and all that snow and ice.

The hotel was small and kind of broken-down, but we didn't mind. Anything for a little relief. We were all worn out. I got out of the Chrysler and headed down the frozen path to the hotel entrance. The winds were whipping the snow into my face and I kept losing my balance and sliding.

I banged on the front door for what seemed like ten minutes. I thought my ears would fall off, that's how cold they were. Finally, an old guy answered the door.

"I'm sorry," he said, "the hotel is closed. The owner just got killed." We heard later the owner had hung himself.

I couldn't believe it. I trudged back through all that

slop wondering if the trip was an omen of what was ahead for me in Toronto. I mean, I'm not that superstitious, but it was like someone was putting a jinx on me even before I joined the new club.

About twenty miles down the highway, we found a motel, but it had taken us five more hours to reach it. After a few hours' sleep, I called Gregory and told him we probably wouldn't make Toronto in time to report later in the day. "That's okay," Gregory said, "We'll find somebody else to back up Plante [Jacques] in case you can't make it." It was a rule that each club is required to dress two goalies for every game.

Coming out of the motel's phone booth, a truck driver told me the roads were clear about fifteen miles from Syracuse. We got everyone together and took off again. It was still pretty bad weather, but we got to the Maple Leaf Gardens Wednesday morning, for the team meeting.

I had been to the Gardens before, but only as a visiting player. In fact, I had to ask a guard for directions to the Leafs' dressing room. In terms of appearance, the Maple Leaf Gardens was nothing like the Spectrum. Let's face it, the Spectrum was only four years old then, and the Gardens was around forty years old.

But when it came to hockey tradition, there was no comparison. The Maple Leaf Gardens and the Forum in Montreal were legendary. They were the two greatest hockey institutions in the world. Every Canadian kid knew what each one of them represented.

As the wife, the kids, Ray, and I walked to the Toronto locker room, I noticed the large framed pictures of some of hockey's greats hanging on the walls.

The players all had one thing in common. They were wearing Maple Leafs' uniforms. I was impressed as hell.

A lot of TV cameramen and reporters were gathered outside the locker room door. "Hey, Bernie," one of them called as we passed. "How about talking to us now?"

"I'll be with you guys right after the meeting," I said. That seemed to satisfy them. They appeared to be pleased with the trade.

It was the same kind of scene inside the locker room. When I opened the door, a lot of guys came right up to me and shook hands. I didn't know any of them well. Davey Keon, the team captain, said the fellows were glad to have me with them.

"We know you're going to help us, Bernie," Davey said.

Then Jacques Plante came over and grabbed my arm. Cripes, Plante was like a god to me. He was my idol. I had been watching him on TV since I was a kid. Now I was on the same team with him. It was then I knew that even though I still felt the hurt over the Philadelphia trade, this trade was going to be the best thing that ever happened to me in hockey.

With Plante around to teach me, it would be like having some gold from the mountain and polishing it. Then, after it was polished, you'd really have something. In this instance, I was the gold, Plante was the polisher. But the question in my mind was whether Plante would take the trouble to polish the gold.

I was very scared about what Plante's reaction would be to me. Would he consider me as just another young goalie trying to take his job away from him?

When I was with the Bruins, I saw some older guys badly resent the younger players. Plante was forty-three, I was twenty-five. He could have really made it hard on me if he wanted to.

And besides all these thoughts, I knew Plante was regarded as a strange guy. He was a loner.

"I have no friends in hockey," Plante used to admit.

He always went his own way off the ice. He never stopped after the game to have a beer with the guys. Plante kept his private life to himself. And with over twenty years in hockey, that was a lot of keeping to himself.

My doubts about Plante's attitude toward me were eased as soon as he spoke to me.

"We'll be playing together, so anything I can help you with just ask," he said warmly.

Although Plante was hardly what you'd call outgoing, he has written what is probably the best book there is on how to play goal.

"Maybe he'll enjoy taking a young goalie under his wing and teaching him the ropes," I thought to myself.

TORONTO AND JACQUES PLANTE, MY HERO

The old man—he knew everything.

Coach Johnny McLellan officially introduced me to the club.

Johnny was liked by nearly everyone. But coaching wasn't for him. After four years as coach with Toronto, Johnny wound up with an ulcer and quit. He is still with the Leafs, but now he is a scout.

The scene in the locker room was kind of weird. The guys were all nice to me, but, like I said, I really didn't know any of them.

And there was one guy, Bobby Baun, whom I actually hated. I couldn't stand to see his face. He was a real mean S.O.B. When he played against us in Philly, he was as vicious as a wolverine in a Yukon winter. Baun had a mug right off the Royal Canadian Mounted Police most-wanted list.

It just goes to show how wrong you can be about people if you don't know a person. Away from the ice, Bobby collects antiques and art. And he has become one of my best friends. I visit him on his farm outside of Toronto every chance I get.

Once when we were hunting caribou in northern Ontario, I told Bobby how I used to feel about him. He just laughed and said:

"Hell, Bernie, I was just doing my job."

Bobby was named coach of the WHA Toronto Toros before the 1975–76 season. If he can get the Toros to play with the same desire he had, they'll do all right.

When we left the meeting, Ricky Ley, one of the Leafs' young defensemen, said he would show us to the house where we would be staying. The house belonged to Marcel Pronovost, a former NHL player who was coaching in the Toronto farm system.

The house was in the suburb of Mississaugua. When we walked in, I knew something was wrong. There were clothes in the closets and some dirty dishes in the sink. We found out later that Larry McIntyre, a defenseman for the Leafs, had been staying there before he was sent to Tulsa.

As hectic as things were, there was still time for a few laughs. Ray and Joan Marella stayed with us a few days, so I thought we should take them out to dinner. The only problem was they didn't bring any dress clothes. Ray had worn hunter's clothes for the trip to Toronto: hunting shirt, jacket, old pants, and boots.

After searching through the closets, we found a suit coat of McIntyre's. When Ray tried the coat on, we all laughed like hell. It looked like a zoot suit the way it hung down over his shoulders. Ray is 5'8" while McIntyre is 6'1".

The women tacked up the sleeves and pants cuffs and we went out like that. Maybe the people who saw Ray in the restaurant thought he was introducing a new style. But we had a good time.

Plante played the game the night we got there. The Flyers were in Toronto that Saturday, but Plante played that game, too, and Toronto won, 4–2.

I was concerned how I would do the first time out with the Leafs.

It wasn't like I was on a team that was close to winning the Stanley Cup. There wasn't that much pressure to produce.

The main thing I worried about was playing behind new guys. What would they do in their own zone? If I caught the puck, where would the defensemen want me to drop it? Except for Baun, Toronto's defensemen then were young—Rick Ley, Jim McKenny, Brad Selwood, Jim Dorey, and Brian Glennie.

The more I thought about it, though, the more I realized that Toronto was a pretty good place to go. They always had goalies such as Johnny Bower and Terry Sawchuk who played my style—stand up, cut down the angles. So I didn't have to do much adjusting.

And besides, the old man, Plante, was there to teach me. Fortunately, we won my first game, 4–2, in Buffalo.

Meanwhile, reaction to the trade in Philly was largely against the Flyers. One fan wrote to Frank Dolson of the *Inquirer,* saying:

> How come it never fails to happen that whenever Philadelphia has a superstar in its ranks it trades him away? This time it is Bernie Parent. He got traded away for a couple of unknowns. So we can officially place Parent with Wilt Chamberlain, Richie Allen, Bob Brown, and others as departed stars from Philadelphia.

I received many letters. Keith Allen wrote thanking me for my "outstanding play for the Philadelphia Flyers" and wishing me the best in the future. Keith wrote:

> You made the remark in the newspaper here that your father told you never to look back and I think that especially in sports this is the right approach, but at times it is hard to do. As I have always told you, I feel that if you continue to work hard you can go on to be one of the best.

Another letter I received was from Bill Putnam, the first president of the Flyers. Part of his letter said:

I make a save on Butch Deadmarsh of Atlanta while
Ed Van Impe and Jimmy Watson look on.

Even stand-up goalies get down — and here I do just that to stop Wayne Cashman. Ken Hodge looks for the rebound.

Left above: Joe Watson, Ed Van Impe and Gary Dornhoefer surround Phil Esposito while I try and "relax."

Left below: It looks suspiciously like Moose has his stick underneath Pete Stemkowski's skates. Probably an optical illusion.

Another kick save (against the Black Hawks) but also a dangerous rebound. Sometimes there is simply no way to stop that from happening.

Left: Two kick saves from different angles. I never knew I looked so graceful!

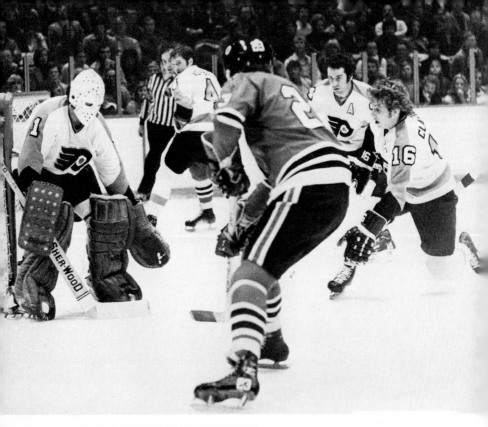

I stopped this one from Chris Bordeleau with my lower left pad. Clarkie, Joe Watson and Barry Ashbee all help out.

Come on fellas! Buffalo fans greeted me last year with this banner.

I wished I were unknown after Rene Robert's goal in overtime beat us in the famous "fog" game of last year. Ed looks on helplessly.

All sorts of strange things happened in the Buffalo playoffs. Here I swing at a bat that decided to pay us a visit. I missed.

MARCEL
VEZINA
PARENT

Back home before the final game, terrific "sign man" Dave Leonardi helped me feel better.

I was most disappointed to learn about the trade because I felt you were a great asset to Philadelphia and that you would have a tremendous future here. You were the "original" Flyer and I'll never forget the contribution you made to our success.

The letter that touched me most was from Bob and Alexis Artese of Drexel Hill, Pennsylvania:

We write to you as two people who have just lost a dear friend and the funny thing is that we have never met you personally. We just finished listening to the Toronto-Buffalo game in which you played and when the announcer said that Bernie Parent saved the game for Toronto it brought tears to the eyes of myself and my wife and even though I am a man of twenty-four I am not embarrassed to admit it.

Further on, they said:

Our life has been built around the Flyers and their future, and with you to fall back on we always had hope. Now the roof has fallen in and hockey in Philadelphia has taken a turn for the worse.

We are not the only ones sorry to see you leave, Bernie. On February 4 at the Flyers-Chicago game there were thirty-five signs or banners hanging up on the Spectrum balcony, all showing real emotion over the loss of a hero. You leaving has left the city in a state of shock.

It was nice to learn how much people in Philadelphia thought of me, but I had to put that behind me and concentrate on helping the Leafs.

That season in Toronto turned out to be better than I thought. We had a winning record (37-33-8), finished fourth in our division, and made the Stanley Cup play-offs.

Although it was a good year, there was only one drawback: Claude saw me play for the first and only time in the NHL. And I lost as Boston bombed us, 9–1.

We had a good play-off series with the Rangers, but they beat us in six games.

Something happened in that series that caused some controversy, none of it very favorable toward me.

About five minutes remained in the game when a brawl started. Vic Hadfield and Jim Harrison were fighting near me, and I guess Hadfield was getting the better of it, so I took off my mask and tried to break them up. When things settled down, Hadfield picked up my mask and threw it into the stands.

The New York fans thought what Hadfield did was pretty funny. Whoever caught my mask refused to return it. I guess Hadfield thought what he did was hilarious, too, even though the damn mask cost a couple hundred dollars. I wonder how he'd like it if I tossed his expensive golf clubs in a pond.

Anyway, I wouldn't continue in the game without the mask. Plante had to come in, and later, some writers actually suggested I was a coward for not playing without the mask. This one New York writer even said I'd never be the same goalie again. In other words, this writer thought I was chicken.

Bull. If I got hit not wearing a mask, I might really never be the same again. It only takes one shot to ruin a goalie not wearing a mask. A goalie is putting his life on the line out there. I wonder if those people who hinted that I had a yellow streak would ask a football player to go on the field without his helmet.

114

One of my weaknesses before coming to Toronto was in clearing the puck. Plante worked with me on that. He was the first goalie to leave the net to clear the puck. I studied his every move when I was on the bench and he was in goal.

One day at practice, I asked the old man how he seemed able to read the shooters so well.

"I've studied them all and have a book on them," Plante said. The next day I started putting together a similar book.

I found out that Plante had more than just a book on shooters. He kept notes on every arena, how to play the boards in each one and how the lighting affected playing goal.

Cripes, the old man—he knew everything.

The only problem in Toronto was Carol never could adapt. It was nothing against Toronto. She would have felt the same about any place except Philadelphia.

Carol said she loved Toronto as a city, and the kids loved to play in the snow. But Carol couldn't warm up to the Toronto fans. She used to say she couldn't understand their casual attitude: instead of cheering for the Leafs, the fans would applaud both teams equally. It seemed that seeing a good game was all that mattered to them.

Next to Bobby Baun, Jim Harrison was my best friend on the Leafs. Jim was a good young centerman who was about to become one of the NHL's best players. Then the Leafs let him get away, to Edmonton of the WHA.

I'll never forget the time Jim, a friend of his, and I went ice fishing on Lake Simcoe near Toronto. We had brought along a case of Cold Duck and it was getting late when this friend of Jim's decided to reach through the hole in the ice for a fish he had caught. The right way to reel in the fish was on the line, but this fellow said, "I'll reach in and grab the fish with my hands."

Well, the guy fell forward and was plunging head-first into the water when I grabbed his legs. Then Jim helped me pull him out. There was only three or four feet of water, but the guy could have drifted away from the hole in the ice and drowned.

The one thing I didn't like about Toronto was the taxes. Canada whacked athletes right where it hurt—in the wallet. Taxes was the one big reason I didn't hesitate to jump to World Hockey.

We had kept our house in Cherry Hill—so we went back there for the summer. We spent a lot of time in Wildwood, New Jersey, because Carol's father, Dick Wilson, had a summer home there.

Everyone calls my father-in-law "Big Dick" and he loves it. Even if he's in a crummy mood, we call him Big Dick and he laughs.

He's the one who got me interested in deep-sea fishing. The first time I went out I got sick as hell, but now I love it. Cripes, what a man Big Dick is. He had open-heart surgery a couple years ago when he was fifty-two. Now he helps me on my boat doing some really hard work, and it doesn't seem to bother him a bit. Not even after a couple beers and a few cigarettes. If I did what Big Dick does, I'd be sweating my tail off.

It was during the summer in Wildwood after my half year in Toronto that I met Howard Casper.

Howard is a Philadelphia attorney who later got into representing many Flyers and other hockey players and pro football players. But at this time, Andy Lacroix was his only athlete client.

When I first talked to Jim Gregory after getting settled in Toronto, he said he would discuss a new contract with me. I had never been represented in contract negotiations before, so Andy thought it might be a good idea for me to meet Howard.

Howard and I sat in the living room of our rented house in Wildwood. The more we talked, the more I realized I had nothing to lose by signing with Howard. But there was one problem: An agent named Mark Stewart had me in a deal where he would get me endorsements. Well, he never got me any, so I asked Howard if I could get out of the deal. Howard assured me that I could do it, legally.

After I signed with Howard, Carol and I started having second thoughts. Ron Smith, my brother-in-law, was there, and he said I might wind up like all those fighters whose managers took all the money they earned. The wife and I started to panic, so we got in the car and started looking for Howard around Wildwood. He had gone back to Andy Lacroix's house, but he wasn't there when we arrived.

By the next day, Carol and I had talked more about signing with Howard and decided to stick with him. We would wait and see what happened. We met with Howard and he saw right away how uneasy I was. So he ripped up the contract and handed the pieces to me.

"All we need is a handshake," Howard said.

I said, "Okay, fine." And that's all we've operated on the last five years.

There is something about Howard that makes you have confidence in him. Even though we've been through some rough times, everything he has done for me has worked out. There have been times we thought about not working with him anymore. He's always so

117

busy with his law practice and representing labor unions that it's tough reaching him by phone. Carol says she's been kept on "hold" by Howard's office half her life. A lot of players got mad and left him because they thought he was too busy to meet their needs. But when we sat down to talk, he explained that he's got more than one client that he's got to satisfy. Sometimes it takes him awhile to do what we want, but it always gets done.

Many people, from owners to writers, don't like Howard. They think he's crude. And sometimes they are right. But that's just his way of dealing with some people. I think people respect and fear him. He just laughs when I mention his "style." He says people don't fear him, but they fear what his clients might do because we trust him and will listen to him.

"I'm rough with some owners," he says, "because all their lives they have dealt in fear with players. The only way to fight fear is to shove it up their ass and give it back to them."

I first saw Howard in action when we went to Toronto in the fall of '71 to renegotiate my contract. I was in the middle of a three-year contract I signed with the Flyers. The Flyers' contract went from $20,000 to $30,000 plus bonuses. During the summer, Gregory offered me a new three-year contract, from $30,000 to $36,000. I told Gregory it wasn't enough and he got in touch with Howard.

We went to Toronto and stayed at the Royal York Hotel. As we were going over a few things, Howard said to me:

"Tomorrow, when we walk into the meeting with Gregory, I want you to sit in the corner, fold your legs, light a cigar, fold your arms, and sit there like Sitting Bull. Whenever I turn to you and say, 'Okay?' you say, 'Okay.' "

I agreed and the next day we walked into Gregory's office in Maple Leaf Gardens. Before anything was said, I tapped Howard on the arm and made a smoking gesture to remind him about the cigar. He gave me a cigar and I walked to a chair in the corner, lit the cigar, and sat down. All this time Gregory and King Clancy are staring at us. Finally Gregory said, "Hello." I just sat there puffing. Clancy, a great old guy who is one of my favorite people in hockey, smiled and said, "How ya' doin', Bern?" I just kept puffing.

Then Howard said, "Gentlemen, I'm here to represent Bernie."

I think Gregory and Clancy knew then that things had changed because I had never been difficult to deal with. I guess they thought they would toss a contract in front of me and I'd sign with no hassle.

Gregory made the offer of thirty, thirty-five, and forty thousand over three years. Howard said, "That's not enough, we're going home." And we got up and walked out.

I'm sure the Leafs were shocked. Here was good old Bernie Parent actually holding out. Howard said a few days later Gregory called him and offered to send the private jet of Harold Ballard, the Leafs' owner, to Philly so Howard could fly back to Toronto and negotiate. Howard rejected the offer.

We went back to Toronto two weeks later, when training camp was under way, and talked again. We were only about $2,000 apart. I had seen the team practicing and felt I was letting them down, so I told

Howard we should take the offer. Howard didn't want me to accept the offer, but I pushed for it.

"Okay, but there's one more thing," Howard said. "With all the taxes they have in Canada we have to be incorporated in the States."

When Howard mentioned being incorporated to Gregory, he looked surprised.

"I can't do that," Gregory said.

I like Gregory, he's a good man, but I guess he didn't know what we were talking about. He said he'd check into it and get back to us.

Now things really got hot. Gregory called Howard and said he had spoken to Clarence Campbell, the NHL president. Campbell said there was an NHL rule that didn't allow you to be incorporated in the States unless you were making $50,000 a year.

That's a lot of bull. There is no such rule. Howard said that with bonuses I would be making $50,000, but Gregory said it had to be in straight salary.

Cripes, Howard even got into an argument with Campbell. Howard said he finally told Cambell to go f—— himself. Campbell told Howard to "get the f—— out of my office" and Howard said, "Fine, because I don't want to sit here talking to an old fart like you." As I said, Howard's style can be rough.

I never signed the Toronto contract, but they paid me that season according to the terms of the contract. Since I hadn't signed, that's why I was free to go to the World Hockey.

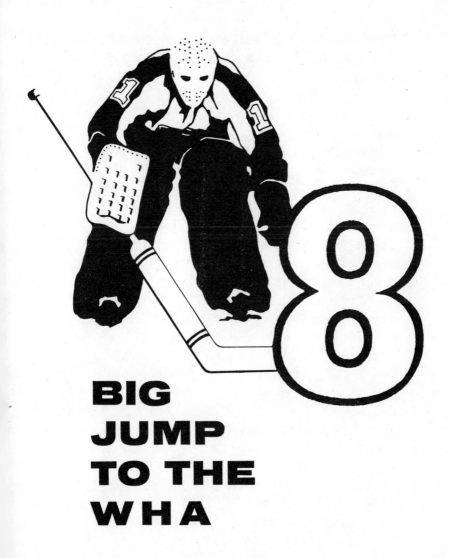

BIG JUMP TO THE WHA

I did for hockey players' salaries what Joe Namath did for the salaries of pro football players.

An event occurred midway in the 1971–72 season that would drastically influence my life.

Even though I hadn't signed with Toronto, I expected to be with the Leafs for a long time. I honestly thought we would settle our contract differences.

Then the new World Hockey Association held its player draft. Early reaction by NHL players to the WHA was curiosity mixed with a "it's a dream, it'll never go" feeling. Starting a new league is more than just a bunch of rich men picking names of players.

When I saw I had been drafted by Calgary, I just smiled and thought, "I don't think I'd like it there. Too cold and too far from home."

Scotty Munro, a successful coach in junior hockey, was heading the Calgary club. He contacted Casper and said he knew he'd have a winner if I played for Calgary. Then Howard and I talked over the Calgary idea. I decided I wouldn't play for Calgary. Howard called Munro and said, "Scotty, Bernie wants to play in the league, but he won't play in Calgary. I'm going to the league and see what I can do about it."

Munro was mad as hell and told Howard only over his dead body would I play for another WHA team.

Howard went to the league and said we would sign now if I was assigned to the Miami franchise. Then we began negotiating with Miami.

Herb Martin was the Miami owner and Lester Patrick was the general manager.

Martin had this unique idea for an arena. He was

building an office complex. The four buildings formed a square and inside the square would be the arena. Martin also had a unique nickname for this team: Screaming Eagles. It was almost as bad as the Golden Seals. Maybe it was worse.

Anyway, Martin sent Patrick to see Howard in Philly. Patrick offered something like $75,000 a year for five years.

"Get back to me when you're serious," Howard told Patrick.

Martin and Patrick then worked out a deal with Howard for about $750,000 over five years plus a house, boat, car, clothes, the whole works. All the frills were great, but the main reason we signed was the security.

When Howard called us in Toronto, I wasn't home, so he said to Carol, "Sit down. Are you sitting down?" She said she was, then Howard said, "How would you like to play in Miami for over $100,000 a year?" The wife couldn't believe it. A short time ago we were fighting with the Leafs to get $40,000. Now we were being offered more than three times that much.

When someone talks that kind of money, you have to listen. You also have to tell the world to stop spinning for a few minutes and really think. Even though money was my first concern then, I definitely thought the league would make it or I wouldn't have considered it.

And we were having problems with Toronto. But just to be safe, I figured that Plante was forty-three and the Leafs had traded for me as their future goalie. They wouldn't want me to fly the coop. And I thought if the WHA folds, I could still come back to the NHL.

Besides, I always like challenges. No matter what it

may be in life—fishing, water skiing, hunting—I want to do it right. I know I won't do it right every time, but the averages should be on my side.

Going to Miami was frosting on the cake. The whole thing sounded like a good deal, even though the only ice in Miami was in mixed drinks.

The Leafs had a Sunday off, so Howard, the wife, and I flew to Miami. Ironically, Johnny McLellan was on the same plane. His ulcer had been acting up, so the Leafs were sending him to Florida to rest. Seeing me didn't help soothe his ulcers.

We stayed in Miami at the Doral Hotel, in a $100-a-day suite. Cripes, it was the real McCoy.

Howard worked out the final details with Herb Martin, then they held a big press conference. A lot of reporters were there, including some from Montreal and some who were covering baseball spring training. The whole thing was pretty exciting. Bernie Parent and the Screaming Eagles—it sounded like a rock group. But those rock groups make big money and now so was I.

After the press conference a reporter called from a French radio station in Montreal. He started asking me how it felt to be a millionaire. When I tried to answer, I was so excited my mind went blank—I forgot how to speak French! This happened three times, so I handed the phone to Howard. When he picked up the receiver, he heard the reporter say (in English), "Bernie forgot *his* English." The reporter was almost as shaky as I was.

Then we went out to celebrate: steaks and champagne at the Jockey Club, an exclusive private club in Miami. The club overlooks a fabulous marina and we ate and drank and watched the lights on the boats. People were partying on those boats, but they couldn't have been enjoying themselves as much as I was. It was 85° and just beautiful. It was hard for me to imagine that I would be playing hockey for a team called the Miami Screaming Eagles under these tropical conditions.

I wondered whether the girls would come to the games wearing those same skimpy bikinis they paraded around in on the beach. No such luck probably.

The real world of professional hockey seemed to be a thousand miles away—and as it turned out, that's the way it stayed.

By the time I got back to Toronto the news of my signing had been in the papers and on radio and TV. On the plane I had been thinking how everybody would take it. Maybe they would think I was running out on the team.

Toronto management was outwardly mad, as I expected. But I don't think Ballard and Gregory thought the WHA would ever get off the ground, or ice. That kind of thinking really hurt the Leafs, because they were hit as hard as any NHL team by players going to World Hockey, with Ley, Selwood, Jim Harrison, Guy Trottier, and myself all leaving.

In line with their looking down on the WHA, Ballard made statements about not standing in my way if that's the kind of money I was getting. Privately, however, the Leafs wanted to fight me. But they couldn't because I had never signed the contract. Howard says he had all the newspaper clippings and TV tapes of Ballard's statements sent to him. As Howard said, he had the Leafs by the cubes.

Reaction by the Toronto fans surprised me. There were some boos, but generally nobody seemed to mind. As Carol has said, the Toronto fans don't get too excited over anything.

Since Toronto is a workingman's town, I thought some fans might be mad about me making so much money. A lot of men who came to see the games broke their backs as stevedores working on the docks of the St. Lawrence River for maybe $10,000 a year. And here I was grabbing $120,000 a year. Maybe the fans realized it was the fault of Toronto management that I signed with Miami.

The players didn't seem to mind what I had done. In the locker room at my first practice back there were a couple of jokes.

"Can you lend me twenty grand?" Bobby Baun wanted to know.

"Are you taking the whole team out to dinner?" Jim McKenny asked.

Eventually I think the players realized that my going to the new league would help everybody because it would cause a salary war between the two leagues. To show how underpaid hockey players were, Gordie Howe, one of the game's all-time greats, didn't make $75,000 a year until he had been in the NHL almost twenty years.

After I signed, Brad Park, Vic Hadfield, and Rod Gilbert of the Rangers all got contracts worth between $175,000 and $200,000 a year. And a couple months later, Derek Sanderson signed a WHA contract with the Philadelphia Blazers for which he supposedly was to be paid $2.6 million over five years.

But I was the first "name" NHL player to go to the World Hockey.

A lot of people have said I did for hockey players'

salaries what Joe Namath did for the salaries of pro football players. When Namath got his big contract with the New York Jets, the NFL suddenly had to worry about the AFL offering players bigger salaries. So the NFL teams starting paying its players more.

The same thing happened in hockey. When NHL teams started taking the new league seriously, they paid their players big money to keep them from jumping.

The WHA caliber of play wasn't even close to that of the NHL that first year, as I found out firsthand, but I can't say anything against the league.

The WHA is the reason we're all making big money today.

Shortly after I signed with Miami, that big money dream began to look like just that—a dream. Herb Martin ran into zoning problems with his office-arena complex and folded his WHA franchise.

When that happened, Howard and the WHA officials set up a conference call and Howard told them that I would honor my contract if another WHA team that he approved would pick it up. Cripes, Gary Davidson, the WHA president, couldn't thank us enough.

That's when Jim Cooper got into the WHA. Cooper was an attorney from Atlantic City, New Jersey, who had been a Flyers' fan. A friend of his who was involved with the WHA's New York franchise asked him if he'd be interested in starting a Philadelphia team. Cooper contacted Bernie Brown, a Vineland, New Jersey, trucking magnate. Brown, a friend of Cooper's, said he'd go in, and in a couple days the Philadelphia Blazers were under way.

One of Cooper's positions was he would only get

involved if I would play for Philadelphia. Asking me if I wanted to return to Philly was like asking Henry Kissinger if he likes traveling. And after I met Cooper, I knew the deal was set.

Jim Cooper is one of the super people I have met in sports. He is a real gentleman, a man who really cared about the players. I think Cooper tried to do the best he could for us under difficult circumstances.

Before our Blazers' season opened Cooper and I went fishing. It was a beautiful sunny day, the ocean was calm, and I was having a relaxing time.

Then Cooper started talking about this innovation he had for WHA games. Usually Cooper and I got along great, but this time, the more he talked, the madder I got. As I was sipping a beer, Cooper said:

"I think we should have sudden-death overtimes in tie games. Five minutes of sudden death and then, if the game is still tied, we'll have a shootout. You know, like penalty shots. First a player from one team shoots at the goalie, then the other team gets a chance. The first team to score wins."

As Cooper and I talked, I really got ticked off. I could just see it: Play sixty minutes of hard hockey, then an overtime, and then a shootout! The man had to be goofy. He didn't realize the pressure goaltenders were under. A couple "shootouts" and the hospitals would be crowded with goalies, batting their heads against the walls. While they were still wearing their masks!

Finally, I jumped up and shouted, "It's no good, your idea is no good. Too much pressure on the goalies!"

Cooper's plan reminded me of an idea Stu Nahan was once spreading. Stu was one of the Flyers' original

128

announcers. He also did an afternoon kiddie TV show. Stu was Captain Philadelphia. From hockey to Captain Philadelphia: What a contrast!

Anyway, Stu had been a hockey goaltender as a youngster. He is now a successful sportscaster in Los Angeles and still plays in the "old-timers" games at the Forum, home ice of the L.A. Kings.

Stu kept telling people that a white puck should be used in hockey games to make the game more exciting. Imagine trying to follow a white puck against the background of white uniforms and ice!

I'm told that when Stu interviewed Gump Worsley, the goalie who played in the NHL until he was forty-four or forty-five, Stu suggested the white puck idea. Gump was speechless and his eyes grew as wide as the St. Lawrence River.

I'm glad Stu was only joking. For a while I thought he may have seen too many Three Stooges films on his *Captain Philadelphia* show.

We had to play in Philadelphia Civic Center Convention Hall, an old building in West Philadelphia near the University of Pennsylvania campus. The building has been kept in good condition, but hockey was never meant to be played there. Basketball, yes; ice shows, yes; but hockey, no. They had to install an ice surface, which led to our unforgettable Friday-the-thirteenth opener when the ice cracked and the game was postponed. The playing area was too narrow, making a goaltender feel like he was at the end of a tunnel when the other team came down the ice. And our dressing rooms were on the second floor. Again, they tried like hell to make it nice. The dressing room, like the entire interior of the building, was repainted with **bright** orange and yellow, the team colors. Lorraine Cooper, Jim's attractive wife, picked the colors because they are her favorites.

The summer before the Blazers opened was lively, with the club signing Johnny McKenzie and Derek Sanderson. McKenzie was signed for about $100,000 a year as player-coach. "Pie" had been a big part of the Bruins' two Stanley Cup winners. He was thirty-five when the Blazers signed him, but he was still a pesky, hustling player who would help a team.

Sanderson was, well, he was the Turk. He was shocked when the Blazers offered him the $2.6 million. He really didn't want to leave the Bruins, but finally he figured what the hell, if they want to pay that kind of money, who am I to refuse.

Cripes, when the Turk came to Philly during the summer for his signing press conference, you'd have thought Paul Newman or Robert Redford was in town. The Blazers held a fancy luncheon for him and even transported everybody by bus from the Bellevue-Stratford Hotel to JFK Plaza in center city where the Turk autographed the book he had out. They even had a police escort for the short trip. One of the cops told Derek he was involved when the Bruins climbed into the Spectrum stands during a 1970 Flyers' game.

"You stepped on me," the cop said. "But now I'm getting a Blazers' season ticket."

Derek should have stepped on more people. Maybe then the Blazers' would have had bigger crowds.

The Turk really had a good time that day. He loved the attention, but that's what Cooper and the Blazers got him for—to promote the team. Some of the Turk's best lines that day included: "I won't change my lifestyle [coming to supposedly sedate Philadelphia]. In fact, I'll increase it because now I can afford it," and "How could Alan Eagleson jeopardize Bobby Orr's career by asking him to play against the Russians? Some stiff Russian from Siberia would love to hurt Bobby Orr." (Orr had recently undergone surgery).

The Blazers also signed Andy Lacroix, so we had the nucleus of a good team. We could have used a few experienced defensemen, but Cooper and Bernie Brown had spent so much for the Turk, Andy, McKenzie, and me that they had to watch the bank account. I'm not knocking the defensemen we had, guys such as Ron Plumb, Jim Cardiff, and Irv Spencer. They tried, but there were many nights I felt awfully alone out there.

Training camp was held in Sherbrooke, Quebec. None of the NHL players could work out with the team until October 1 because that's when the NHL contracts expired.

The main memory I have from that 1972 camp was very few people believed we were really a team or that the league would get started. People would laugh at us and say we belonged back in the NHL. When we'd travel, people would stare and ask, "Who are you guys?" Oh, they'd recognize Sanderson, McKenzie, or me, but they still didn't know who the Philadelphia Blazers were.

On one trip to Springfield, Massachusetts, for an exhibition game, Sanderson decided to order Chinese food after the game. Well, he ordered $125 worth of food. When they brought it, there was so much we had to get another room just for the food.

The summer and camp had been such a hectic time that we were all looking forward to opening night. A good crowd turned out—over seven thousand—but as we and the New England Whalers warmed up we noticed something was wrong with the ice. It was soft in spots and looked like it might crack.

We finished warm-up and trudged up the steps to our dressing room with me wearing my orange "double zero" sweater. A few minutes later, someone came and said, "The game's off. The ice cracked under the Zamboni machine."

Cripes, what an omen! My "double zero" number was intended to signify the number of goals I would allow. But I used to tell people it was for when a puck would get past me. I'd look around and say, "Oh-oh." That's how I felt when the ice cracked. Oh-Oh, what's going to happen next?

Later, we were told there was a problem with the way the pipes under the ice were packed. Cooper went out to try apologizing over the public address system, but some jerks in the crowd started throwing souvenir pucks at him. The Turk tried talking to the people, asking them to come back "even though the parking ain't too good," but the fans weren't happy. I couldn't blame them. It was a terrible way for a new team in town to start.

The ice breakdown completed a busy day for me. Carol had given birth to our daughter, Kim, earlier in the week while we were finishing training camp in Canada. They were to come home from West Jersey Hospital in Camden on Friday, the day of the Blazers' opener, but the doctor, Eugene Haag from Haddonfield, New Jersey, was a hockey fan. He knew it would be hard for me to move Carol and the baby while getting ready for a game. So he said they should stay in the hospital until Saturday.

I had gotten home Thursday, but wanted to go deer

hunting Friday morning with Ray Marella. It would be my last chance to hunt deer that year.

As luck would have it, we got a deer and had to track it. I called Carol, told her I was sorry, but I wouldn't get to the hospital until Saturday. Carol wasn't too pleased. In fact she told me what I could do with my deer. But said she would listen to the game on the radio. She forgot that the Blazers' games weren't on the radio at that time, so she didn't know what happened with the ice until Saturday morning when she asked a nurse for the score. The nurse told her about the game being postponed.

As if the bad ice on opening night wasn't bad enough, injuries started piling up. McKenzie had broken his arm in camp, a couple games into the season Sanderson hurt his back, then I broke my foot during the first game Carol saw. Early in the delayed home opener against Cleveland I stopped a shot with my right skate. It hurt like hell, but I finished the first period. Then I was taken to the hospital, where the foot was X-rayed and the broken bone was discovered.

That trip to the hospital to X-ray my foot wasn't my only hospital visit of the year.

In a few days, I was back in again. But this time by choice, not chance.

I had been doing a lot of reading about the dangers of cancer. In one magazine a doctor wrote that men who were circumcised had a lot less chance of contracting cancer than men who weren't.

It started me wondering. I mean, I'm really squeamish when it comes to hospitals. Even going to see friends who are patients makes me feel light-headed. But I'm also squeamish about things like cancer. Far more squeamish than I am about hospitals.

Since I was born to wear a Catholic cross, not a Jewish mezuzah, around my neck, I wasn't circumcised. Maybe now I should wear a mezuzah because Howard keeps telling me that now I'm more like a Jew than he is.

And although many male babies are circumcised today for medical reasons—whether or not they're Jewish—that certainly wasn't the custom in Canada thirty years ago.

But after what I read, and figuring I had some time on my hands, I decided to let the surgeon take the matter in his hands.

I told Howard and Jim Cooper of my plans. I think they were ready to rush me to the nearest rabbi for conversion to Judaism.

They both warned me how painful circumcision was supposed to be, although I'm sure neither of them remembered from experience.

The doctors who had examined my broken foot had advised me I couldn't step on the ice for at least four weeks. Even to practice.

So when Dr. Louis Keeler, the surgeon who operated, said I would be all healed in ten days, I foresaw no problems.

Maybe I should have suspected trouble the moment I entered a good Catholic Hospital like our Lady of Lourdes in Camden for an operation one generally associates with Jewish males.

I was in a room with three other guys and they were all teasing me about my impending surgery.

One of my roommates cracked, "Well, it won't be long now."

I kind of hoped he was referring to the length of time I had to wait for the operation.

Really, I didn't see anything too funny in what I was about to go through. Especially when I recalled what Howard and Jim had warned me about the pain I'd probably suffer.

But once the operation was over, it was my turn to laugh. Oh, I ached all right, but it was a real relief. Now it was my turn to toss out the one-liners.

When Howard came to visit me, I said, "Howard, I don't want you to eat any ham, pork, or bacon now that I'm a rabbi."

And I teased Jim by telling him then that the doctor had to use fifteen stitches to close my wound. Fifteen stitches an inch apart, that is. . . . Yeah, I was only joking.

What wasn't so hilarious, though, was the night Carol and some of her family came up to see me.

They brought along a copy of *Playgirl* and did a pretty good ribbing job of their own.

Another thing that didn't strike me as funny was something that happened after I got out of the hospital. That's when I started thinking I may have been jinxed because this nice Catholic boy went to a nice Catholic hospital for a nice Jewish operation.

Since it was hunting season, I thought it would be okay if I put a plastic cover over the cast on my foot and went out with Ray Marella to try to bag a deer.

Bernie Brown got wind of my hunting escapades and really flipped out. My circumcision wasn't healed, so Brown reasoned that if I could walk in the woods, I could practice on the ice. He threatened to fine me, but never did.

After I returned to the team December 1, I played in every game. It didn't bother me too much because I was being paid a lot of money and our backup goalie,

Marcel Paille, was forty years old and really not up to playing a lot.

I think the thing I missed most in those WHA games was the NHL atmosphere—the full arenas and the noise. Most of the time the Blazers were playing before three to four thousand people. It was hard getting up for those games. I wouldn't have cared if they booed if they only made some sound. Maybe they should have had a record ready, and whenever you made a move you'd hear "Boo!"

About the middle of November, Cooper and Brown split up, with Cooper pulling out of the club. The players hated to see Cooper go because he had been close to the team. About the only times we saw Brown were at games.

Brown held a meeting with the team that shocked everybody. We were used to strange things happening with the Blazers. And we had even grown used to Phil Watson's screaming sessions. Watson was a former New York Rangers' coach who had been brought in to help McKenzie coach and also run the hockey operation in the front office. I don't recall any player ever having much nice to say about Watson. The odd thing was he didn't seem to mind. He once told someone that when he died, he hoped he would be buried face down so all the hockey people could come by and kiss his butt.

The main idea of Brown's meeting was that he didn't care about contracts, that to him contracts were made to be broken. Brown was a big, imposing man, about fifty years old, so when he said he planned to run the hockey club like his trucking business, we all believed him. It's my belief that as soon as he and Cooper parted, Brown decided to unload the team.

Indications of Brown's decision were the way he forced Sanderson out and tried to get me to break my contract. Derek said he was ready to resume playing in mid-season, but we kept hearing the club wouldn't let him suit up. Finally, Derek and his attorney, Bob Woolf of Boston, settled for about $300,000 and Derek returned to the Bruins.

The Blazers' attempt to get rid of me centered around continued aggravation. For one thing, I wouldn't get paid on time. The Blazers also fooled around at taking care of medical expenses they had agreed to pay. The embarrassment upset Carol. We kept getting the bills for Kim's birth. Howard would turn them over to the club, but nothing would happen.

Around March of '73 Howard met with Dick Olson, a man Brown had brought in from Chicago to run the club. Olson had been successful selling hospital supplies, which was the right kind of background for the Blazers.

Olson tried to settle the problem of my guaranteed money by asking Howard to accept Bernie Brown's personal guarantee. Howard and I agreed this was risky business, but when Howard passed our answer along to the Blazers, they seemed insulted. Cripes, right in our contract it read:

> . . . The guarantee must be satisfactory to Howard J. Casper, Esquire, in his sole discretion. If, for any reason, Howard J. Casper, Esquire, is not satisfied with the guarantee presented by employer, this contract shall become null and void, at his option."

The Blazers' behavior puzzled us. As Howard said, even Gary Davidson, the WHA president, wouldn't accept an owner's personal guarantee because of the legal technicalities involved.

Howard continued to try talking with Olson, but he kept saying he felt we were holding a gun to his head. I couldn't believe it! They wouldn't guarantee me my money. I kept playing, but we were holding a gun to their heads.

We finally decided I would play one play-off game against Cleveland, but if the problem wasn't resolved by the next morning, that was it. No money, no Bernie Parent in the nets.

Howard never heard from Olson, so he called him in Chicago at his home. Olson repeated his "gun-to-the-head" nonsense and said he expected me to be in Cleveland for the second play-off game. Howard told Olson where he could shove one of his forceps. Howard then contacted Gary Davidson.

Howard and I were to play golf on a Saturday morning. I had packed a suitcase in case I was going to Cleveland. From his car Howard called Davidson in Boston. Davidson kept us waiting about twenty minutes, then said, "Look, I'm not getting involved in this. It's none of my business."

We were sitting in Howard's Mercedes convertible in the driveway of his Bryn Mawr, Pennsylvania, home. We looked at each other and couldn't believe it. Here was the WHA president saying a contract crisis concerning one of the new league's top players wasn't any of his business.

In our final move before leaving the team, Howard contacted Cooper. We had to go through Cooper because Brown wouldn't speak with us. Howard asked Cooper to tell Brown that I would play for no pay and no guarantee as long as the Blazers agreed they would not say in a lawsuit that I waived my right to the money by playing. Legally, we had made a demand for the money. If I then played without receiving the money, the Blazers could say I had waived my right to it.

On Sunday, Howard reached Olson in his room at Philadelphia's Marriott Motor Hotel. Again Olson declined our offer and then said I would never play for the Blazers again. He also said the players didn't want me back.

The newspaper stories backed what Olson said. Johnny McKenzie was really hard on me, saying I acted like I needed help going to the bathroom. Carol was more upset with what McKenzie said than I was because I figured he was speaking after a game without having time to think.

After I left the team, I offered to meet with the players and explain my reasons for leaving. Howard sent telegrams to all the players, but the club management found out about my offer and told the players if they attended the meeting they would be fined and would be through.

Just to complete the sad situation, someone from the Blazers' organization phoned the leasing company that owned my Mark IV and asked that the car be picked up on the street. They tried sending Jerry Rafter, our good friend and Blazers' personnel director, for the car, but Jerry refused.

As I expected, I took a lot of criticism. Stan Hochman wrote in the Philadelphia *Daily News* that I deserved "equal amounts of pity and scorn." When Stan asked at our press conference about me abandoning ship at such a vital time, I smiled and said, "I'm a good swimmer."

That remark wasn't meant to be smart. I felt rotten

about what the effects of my leaving would do to the players, who had overcome more obstacles than a Marine recruit to make the play-offs. But there comes a time in life when you have to stand up for yourself. The owner was doing everything possible to make life miserable for me. I love the game, but not enough to play for nothing.

As if I didn't feel bad enough, the day after our press conference at a center city Holiday Inn I got the call from home that my mother had died from a massive hemorrhage.

Yves Archambault, a rookie in his first pro season, took my place and played well in a tough situation. But Cleveland won in four straight. About one month later, the Blazers were sold to people in Vancouver.

The Blazers were gone, thank goodness, but some bitter feelings remained. I did smooth over resentment involving the team by meeting with such players as Ron Plumb and Jim Cardiff over a few beers. When they heard my side of the story, I think they agreed I did the right thing.

Influencing the public's opinion wasn't as easy. We received many letters from angry fans. Some were so cruel they had Carol in tears. Business executives wrote that walking out on the team was a rotten thing to do, that they would never do that to their company. Maybe not, but how many businessmen who discovered they wouldn't be paid would tell their company, "That's okay, I'll work my tail off for you anyway."

Shortly after the Blazers' season ended, the wheels started turning for me to return to the Flyers.

9

MY COMEBACK TO THE FLYERS

Right away they knew: Kate Smith was there. In person!

After the bitter parting with the Blazers, I had two options:

1. Stay in the WHA with another team. The New York team was very interested in picking up my contract. Or:

2. Go back to the NHL. Toronto still thought it had my WHL rights, but Howard maintained I was a free agent.

I knew I wouldn't play in Toronto again. The only NHL team I wanted to play for was the Flyers, but I wondered if they would have me.

After I was traded by the Flyers there had been several incidents that might affect their feelings toward me. The problems weren't with the players, but with the front office.

During the season I played with the Blazers, I dropped by the Flyers' office at the Spectrum. Some people there reacted as if I were carrying the plague. Their reaction really ticked me off and I quickly left.

After one Blazers' game, a Philly writer led me into blasting Flyers' management. I said they would never go anywhere until they got first-class management. Well, the writer caught me at a bad time. I was feeling down, and as soon as I saw the story, I regretted what I had said.

Shortly after the Blazers' season ended, I asked Howard to check with the Flyers and see if they would want me. Evidently they did, although at first Mr. Snider was cool to the idea. The problem was with Toronto. Gregory took a tough stance when Howard called, saying I had to play for the Leafs. But Howard knew Gregory was just bluffing. If Toronto didn't make a deal for me with the Flyers, I'd go to another WHA team and the Leafs would get nothing out of the deal.

That summer my comeback with the Flyers was arranged in two stages. First, the Leafs received the Flyers' first amateur draft choice, who turned out to be defenseman Bob Neely. In exchange the Flyers got Toronto's second draft pick. The Flyers used that pick to select Larry (Izzy) Goodenough, who looked like a good defenseman for us.

The second and final part of the deal caused more controversy. The Flyers had to send Doug Favell to Toronto.

As much as I wanted to return to the Flyers, I hated to see them have to give up Favvy. I knew how much he liked Philly and how hard it would be for him to leave. I was right. At the press conference announcing Favvy's trade to Toronto, he broke down. Cripes, I really felt bad for him.

The new contract with the Flyers was super. It wasn't as good as my Blazers' contract, but I made up for what the Blazers didn't pay me. And Howard said it made me the highest-paid Flyer.

The four days leading up to my first game back with the Flyers had to be the toughest of my life pressure-wise.

I knew Favell had a lot of fans in Philadelphia and they weren't happy about the trade. To make things even tougher, guess who we were opening against? Right, Favell, and Toronto.

Training camp had its rough spots, too. The Flyers were now training at the University of Pennsylvania. The club figured it would save money by not having to set up camp somewhere in Canada. The club also expected to get more newspaper and television coverage. Before, only the three Philadelphia dailies and a couple in Jersey sent their writers to camp.

Penn's rink is a fairly new three-thousand-seat building on its West Philadelphia campus, near Franklin Field and the Palestra. The rink is next to some overhead railroad tracks, so the hockey writers like to say, "Baseball writers get six weeks in Florida. We get three weeks under the railroad tracks in West Philly."

About the only complaint the club has about Penn's rink is it's always freezing. Hockey rinks are supposed to be cold, but at Penn it's so chilly we have trouble working up a sweat.

Besides more press, radio, and television coverage, training in Philly also gave more fans the opportunity to watch us practice. Freddie closes the morning workouts to the public, but the fans are allowed in for the afternoon scrimmages.

Reaction by many fans to my return matched the temperature at Penn. Some fans used to applaud and boo when I'd miss a shot in workouts. Must have been Favell's fan club.

Our players treated me pretty well. A few made wisecracks about me leaving the Blazers, but I didn't think anybody meant to be vicious. It was just locker room talk, which can be pretty cutting sometimes. Sure, some players were cool toward me, but I think they were just waiting to see how I'd handle myself.

My first game back at the Spectrum was a disaster, to put it mildly. At least on the scoreboard it was terrible. The Rangers scored seven goals against me in twenty-two minutes in our exhibition opener. Freddie knew I wasn't sharp and took me out.

Freddie never says much to the players, and this time was no different. He seemed to be waiting to see how I played.

I did like one comment he made. Freddie and Favvy got along pretty well, although I knew Favvy's goofing around in practice drove Freddie crazy.

I don't think Freddie knew what to expect when the trade was made. He said he had only seen me play a couple times for the Blazers and in the Central League.

When the support for Favvy was mentioned early in training camp, Freddie said:

"I liked Dougie, too, but I know, and I think the players know, that management sometimes has to do things for the team. Having eighteen lovable guys is fine, but if you finish last they aren't so lovable."

The way that exhibition against the Rangers went, our fans probably thought we would finish last. Others might have been upset, but that game didn't really bother me. Oh, it bothered me at the time because nobody likes to get bombed. But I knew I wasn't ready yet. My reflexes weren't ready and I wasn't sharp mentally. And facing the Rangers, with shooters like Rod Gilbert, Jean Ratelle, and Brad Park, is a tough way to start.

By the time the exhibitions were over I felt pretty confident. My timing was back and the team was playing well. Waiting a couple days for the opener against Toronto gave me time to think. I tried to be alone as much as possible. I'd take walks in the Jersey fields with Tinker, our German Shepherd. I just liked getting out in the fresh air alone. When I was with Carol and the kids, I'd try to enjoy myself, but usually my mind would wander and I'd find myself thinking about the Toronto game.

On game day, we always have a morning meeting at the Spectrum, where we take a light skate and then go over the night's opponent. I remember Bobby (Chief) Taylor, our backup goalie and a helluva good guy, telling me, "You're the best, go get 'em tonight."

What the Chief said made me feel good. That night before the game, Clarkie and some other players said, "We'll go get 'em for you."

The club really made a big production out of the opener. All the lights were turned down in the Spectrum, and each player was introduced with a spotlight on him. It seemed Favell got a bigger hand than I did, but I thought that would happen. I still had a lot to prove to Philly fans.

Before the game I thought that Favell had nothing to lose. The pressure was on me. Dougie and I had been together a long time. We were friendly, we respected each other's ability, but we weren't real close socially. In our position, it was probably impossible for us to be really close friends.

The club had arranged a special surprise for the opener. After the players were introduced, the gates were opened at the end of the Spectrum ice where the Zamboni machine enters the ice, and a carpet was rolled out. It was pretty dark, but the fans who were close to the gate could see an organ being pushed out on the carpet. Right away they knew: Kate Smith was there. In person!

As I'm sure almost every hockey fan knows by now, Kate Smith is our good-luck charm. When her recording

146

of "God Bless America" is substituted for the National Anthem, we hardly ever lose. Seeing her in person gave us all a charge.

Not many Toronto players knew what was going on, but Dougie knew all about her good luck for the Flyers. When he saw her he said, "Oh-oh, we're in trouble."

Dougie's fears came true. We won 2–0 with Terry Crisp and Billy Barber scoring. That Crispie would score the first goal was weird. Before the game Dougie was interviewed on television and when Hugh Gannon of Channel 10 asked which Flyer shooter he feared the most, Dougie laughed and said, "Not Terry Crisp, that's for sure." Guys are always kidding Crispie about his shot. Crispie said when Favvy was still with the Flyers, he would drop his glove and dare Crispie to shoot at his bare hand.

When the game ended, I felt as if someone had just lifted the Spectrum scoreboard off my shoulders. When the writers asked how I felt, I said, "It was just like George Foreman and Joe Frazier going at each other." I was glad it was over.

The next day I read that Freddie said I was the greatest goalie he had ever coached. Freddie had coached Plante and Gilles Villemure. How he could decide I was the best after one game I don't know, but that's Freddie. I suspect he was trying to keep my confidence up.

What Freddie said must have helped, because we shut out the Islanders 6–0. We won our first four games, but lost the next three. Then we won four in a row, including two more shutouts. After ten games we were leading the West Division and starting to believe how good we were.

The fourth shutout was something special for us. We beat Chicago 1–0. Tony Esposito was in goal for the Black Hawks. Esposito is one of the best goalies in hockey, so anytime you beat him by 1–0 it's a great feeling.

Again, Billy Barber scored a big goal for us. It was a rough game, and we had to kill four penalties in the first period before Barber scored from about thirty-five feet. One of these days, and I hope it's soon, Billy will get the recognition he deserves as one of hockey's best left-wingers. Maybe his problem is he isn't real colorful. He doesn't have a shot like Richard Martin and he doesn't play in New York like Steve Vickers. But to me, he's the best all-around left-winger in hockey. Billy hasn't been a pop-off type guy, although Frank Lewis, our trainer, told me that when Billy was a rookie he was very self-confident and would gripe a little. Once on a flight Frank told him, "If this plane we're on crashed, you'd be the first to complain."

I think Billy has matured a lot. And he scored at least thirty goals his first three seasons in the NHL. He does have a terrible nickname though. It's "Arnie," and he's not named after Arnold Palmer. Billy's nickname comes from the pig on *Green Acres,* the old TV show. When Clarkie tries to get Billy's attention on the ice, he'll yell "Arnie!"

Normally a 1–0 lead against Chicago is as safe as taking off for the moon in a dune buggy. The Black Hawks have great playmakers in Stan Mikita and Pit Martin and dangerous scorers in Dennis Hull, Jim Pappin, Cliff Koroll, and Dick Redmond, but our defense did a super job.

In the dressing room when the writers asked me

148

about the four shutouts in ten games, I kept telling them it wasn't just me. Freddie and Mike Nykoluk had us playing our system, and I was only getting four or five tough shots a game.

Beating Chicago like that was a good send-off to our deer hunting trip the next day. We were excused from practice, so I was taking Joe Watson deer hunting. After the game, I hollered loud enough so Joe could hear. "I'm going to shoot Joe and put him on the hood of the car." Thank goodness, Joe laughed.

Like Gary Dornhoefer, Ed Van Impe, and me, Joe is an original Flyer. He played one year with Boston before Philly took him in the expansion draft. He's always been a steady defenseman for us, so I was glad to see him get some recognition like playing in the All-Star Game in Chicago and being voted the Flyers' top defenseman for the 1974–75 season.

One year when the Flyers were training in Ottawa, Joe almost quit hockey. He came to camp out of shape. One morning during a workout the guys looked around and there was Joe leaning over the boards, parting with his breakfast or late-night snack.

Joe really missed his wife, Marianne. He said he was going back to his hometown, Smithers, British Columbia, and find a job. Keith Allen and others tried to talk him out of leaving. Finally, his good friend and defensive partner Eddie Vam Impe called Bobby Orr at the Bruins' training camp in London, Ontario. Orr had been best man at Joe's wedding. Orr called Joe and convinced him to stay.

Joe takes a lot of kidding from the team, but only because everybody likes him. He's a great team man, the kind who is always talking it up on the bench and in the dressing room. Among his nicknames are Thundermouth and Pumpkin. Joe's black, curly hair is similar to Bill Flett's poodle, which is named Pumpkin. Flett was on our first Stanley Cup team, then was traded to Toronto.

The good start by the team and me was the greatest thing that could have happened. I don't think we were ever out of first place that season. For a while, I imagine a lot of people were waiting for us to fold, but we were getting balanced scoring from Clarkie, Ricky MacLeish, Barber, and Ross Lonsberry. Dave Schultz got twenty goals, and Simon Nolet, who could never make Freddie believe he should be playing regularly, scored nineteen.

Our defense was just super, with Eddie, Joe, Barry Ashbee, Moose Dupont, Tom Bladon, and Jimmy Watson. Jimmy is Joe's younger brother. Keep an eye on him. He'll be one of the best. Our defense, including the forwards, was the reason my average looked so good and I got those twelve shutouts. The forwards and defensemen played Freddie's "team" system so beautifully that I rarely saw more than twenty-five shots a game.

Probably our biggest win was one week before the season ended. Not only did we clinch the West Division championship, but we finally beat Boston. It's hard to believe now, but until we beat the Bruins, 5–3, we had an 0–23–4 streak of failure against them dating back to the Flyers first year in the NHL.

Knowing we could clinch the division title, the club had placed black and orange balloons in the Spectrum rafters. When time ran out in the game, the balloons floated to the ice and champagne flowed in the dressing room. I'm sure many people, especially those from Boston, thought we were celebrating too early, but when we beat the Bruins for the Stanley Cup, a lot of us looked back to that win as proof we could beat Boston.

About the only thing left in the final week before the play-offs was winning the Vezina Trophy. Tony Esposito and I were in a helluva race for the Vezina, which goes to the team allowing the fewest goals.

One thing Freddie and I don't agree on is the importance of the Vezina. He calls it the worst trophy ever invented because he thinks it forces a team to change its style and worry about protecting its goaltender. I think it makes a team play better defense. Freddie was never a goalie, so he can't know how much the Vezina means to us.

Freddie gave me the night off after we beat Boston. I didn't mind because the Boston game was my twenty-eighth straight in the nets and I could use the rest. The Chief played in Minnesota and we won 6–3.

We came home and beat the Islanders 4–0, for my twelfth shutout. On the final weekend of the season, we had to play in Pittsburgh, then come back to the Spectrum against Minnesota. Freddie decided to rest Clarkie, Van Impe, and me in Pittsburgh. Cripes, it had to be the worst game we played all season. The Penguins won 6–1, outshooting us 37–26. The Chief felt terrible. I could see Esposito already posing for pictures with the Vezina Trophy. I'll admit I was upset with Freddie for not letting me play.

In the last game we had a pretty easy time, beating Minnesota 6–2. The win was my forty-seventh, an NHL record. I finished with an average of 1.89. But I went home thinking Esposito had won the Vezina.

The ride home to Cherry Hill that night was very grim. Carol knew I was thinking about the Vezina, so she didn't say much. She knew how important coming back to the NHL and winning the Vezina was to me.

Carol had tears in her eyes as we walked into the house. I think my eyes were misty, too. It just felt so bad to lose the Vezina like that on the final night of the season.

A few minutes after we got home one of the writers called from the Spectrum to tell us Marcel Dionne of Detroit had scored against Esposito in the final minute. We thought it was a joke at first, but the writers insisted they weren't kidding. Chicago won 7–4, but Esposito and I had tied for the Vezina. Geez, I was happy! The team had finished first and I had proven something to everybody.

"Tell Dionne I'll take him fishing," I told the writers. Now that Dionne plays for Los Angeles, maybe he can take me fishing. Somewhere around Acapulco or Hawaii would be nice.

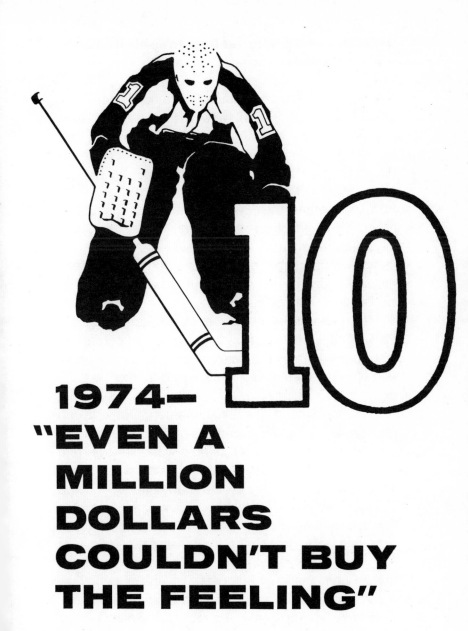

10

1974– "EVEN A MILLION DOLLARS COULDN'T BUY THE FEELING"

If people want pretty skating, they should go to the Ice Capades.

A Stanley Cup play-off against the Atlanta Flames—that was our first assignment if we were to win our first cup.

The Flames were a great success story. In only their second year in the league, they finished fourth in the West Division. They were only four points behind Los Angeles in third, and nine ahead of Pittsburgh.

Cliff Fletcher, their general manager, and Bernie (Boom Boom) Geoffrion, their coach, had done a super job putting the team together. Even in their first year they gave us trouble because the Boomer had them playing a defensive, grind-it-out style. And they all worked their tails off.

The Flames reminded me of our early teams in Philly. They didn't have many big goal scorers, although young guys like Tom Lysiak, Jacques Richard, and Curt Bennett looked like they'd become top players.

Lysiak plays a lot like Clarkie—smart, always taking charge. And he's tough. Richard has a great shot, but Eddie Van Impe and Dorny would work him over and take his mind off scoring goals. Bennett is a big guy who reads a dictionary on the road. He also studied Russian. We ought to get him. The way Freddie likes Russian hockey, Bennett could help him translate.

Atlanta's biggest strength was its goaltending. Like Favvy and me, Phil Myre and Dan Bouchard gave them a solid combination in the nets. It's kind of eerie how much Myre and Bouchard ressemble Favvy and me. Myre is a stand-up goalie, like me, while Bouchard has a more colorful style, like Favvy. Through its first two seasons, Atlanta always knew it would get respectable goaltending.

We felt if we played our game in the play-offs, we would beat Atlanta. But we also knew that if Myre or Bouchard got hot, we might have a tough time. I'm sure the Flames were counting on their goaltending as their ace.

Myre played well in the first two games at the Spectrum, but we won 4–1 and 5–1. Rich MacLeish had the hat trick in the 5–1 win. Ricky is something in the play-offs. It often looks as if he's just floating around on the ice, but that's just his style. He probably has the most natural talent of anyone on our team. And his wrist shot is the best in the league. You never know when he's going to release the shot. When he does, zip! It's past you.

Ricky had a big goal for us in the third series game at Atlanta. He let one go that seemed to hit the post and bounce out, but the referee, Dave Newell, ruled it a goal.

Bouchard went crazy. He swung his stick at the glass protecting the goal judge, then skated over and charged the officials. Everyone thought he bumped the officials, but all he got was a misconduct. Anyway, we won 4–1, and were in command of the series, three games to none.

With a Saturday night off, we tried to relax by going out for a good dinner, then visiting Underground Atlanta. During the regular season, the team stays in the Marriott Motor Hotel, but for the play-offs we switched to the Regency Hyatt House, which is a couple blocks from the Marriott.

Both hotels are in the downtown area, not far from

the Underground, which is a collection of shops, restaurants, and nightclubs. Lester Maddox, the former governor of Georgia, had a place there where you could buy souvenirs. Sometimes he'd even be in the shop, signing autographs. I hear he sings. Maybe the Flames should hire him as their answer to our Kate Smith.

Changing hotels in Atlanta was Freddie's idea, to separate the players from the press and fans. The change worked fine, except that Freddie was almost separated from his wallet and health. I wish I could tell what really happened that night, but all we know is Freddie was late for the team meeting Sunday morning so Mike Nykoluk went to his room and found Freddie in bed beat up. Freddie couldn't remember what happened. Since he's such a loner, no one was with him to get the true story.

My guess is that Freddie was having a few beers by himself in a bar and some guys found out who he was. Maybe they made a few not-so-choice remarks about the Flyers, then roughed him up. The way downtown Atlanta is deserted at night, he could have walked back to the hotel without anybody noticing.

Something like your coach being beaten up could upset some clubs. But even though we felt bad, we knew we had a job to do. The club sent Freddie home to rest and Mike took over behind the bench. The Flames gave it a helluva try, taking a 3–0 lead. Then Schultzie got into a fight with Bryan Hextall. I don't know if Dave was trying to get us going or what, but it worked. Twelve seconds later Moose Dupont scored for us.

The game went into overtime after goals by Dorny and Tom Bladon tied it. Schultzie, the last guy the

Atlanta fans wanted to see score, took a perfect pass from Clarkie and beat Myre to give us a 4–3 win and a spot in the semifinals against the Rangers.

The Rangers' series was everything we expected: close, tough, and full of bad feelings. The New York fans hate us and Emile Francis, the Rangers' general manager-coach, thinks we are the worst things to set foot on earth since Attila and his Huns. Francis has every right not to like us, but I've felt he has a lot to say for the general manager of a team that hasn't won a Stanley Cup since 1940.

We won the series opener at the Spectrum, 4–0. The Rangers had only nineteen shots. The second game was special because we were leading 1–0 in the second period when Eddie Van Impe scored. Geez, Eddie hardly ever scores goals. They told us later it was his first goal in thirty-four Stanley Cup games. During the season he had scored only twice.

Freddie keeps saying Eddie is valuable because he knows his limitations. Offensively, Eddie knows he can't rush the puck like Orr, so he usually just dumps it out of our zone. When Eddie was team captain, the writers used to call him Captain Clear.

Eddie is also valuable because he'll do anything to help us win, whether it's blocking shots or working somebody over in front of the net. Eddie also has a sense of humor. When Gene Hart, our broadcaster, asked me after we beat Buffalo for the cup what it means to have Eddie playing in front of me, I said, "It means you get screened a lot." Eddie laughed. He knew I was only kidding.

Eddie's goal against the Rangers was one of those crazy bouncers. As he does so well, Eddie just tried to put the puck on the net. Instead, it bounced off Rod Seiling's stick and went in over Ed Giacomin's shoulder. Giacomin didn't think it had crossed the line, but the judge turned on the light.

Giacomin was mad as hell, just like Bouchard was in Atlanta. Giacomin swung his stick at the glass protecting the judge. I couldn't blame Giacomin. There have been times I felt we got screwed on calls. You get so angry you just strike out at the nearest thing.

We needed Van Impe's goal because by early in the third period we were only leading 2–1. That's when we got one of the biggest plays of the series.

New York had a power play, which was the NHL's best that season. Bobby Rousseau passed the puck to Pete Stemkowski at the left point, but Stemkowski slipped. Suddenly, Ross Lonsberry swooped in, took the puck, and skated in on Giacomin. Brad Park tried to intercept Roscoe, but failed. Roscoe pulled Giacomin, then put in a backhander that gave us a 3–1 lead. We won it 5–2.

Roscoe's aggressiveness was typical of our team. Some people probably thought he should have played it safe, killing the penalty with us leading 2–1. But he said it never entered his mind to be cautious. He saw the loose puck and immediately thought of scoring.

People knock us for all the penalties we take and sometimes they're right. We do take some needless penalties. But we've also got some great penalty killers, like Clarkie, Roscoe, Rick MacLeish, Billy Barber, Dorny, and Terry Crisp. The way our team plays, our penalty killers get a lot of practice.

We've become like the Bruins when they had Eddie Westfall and Derek Sanderson. They were always thinking offense when they were shorthanded. I'm sure some teams get a little nervous when they have a power play against us. Sometimes the fans aren't sure which team has the manpower advantage.

Now we had to go to New York. As our record showed, Madison Square Garden wasn't our favorite place to play. We always had trouble there, even in the old Garden. Sure the fans are noisy, but we should have done better there. The "Bern-nie! Ber-nie! Ber-nie!" chant by our fans is their answer to the "Ed-die! Ed-die! Ed-die!" of New York fans when Giacomin makes a good save.

For a while in game three, it looked as if we finally had broken our jinx. We led 3–1, but then all our penalties cost us and New York won 5–3, outshooting us by 39–15. Freddie was really ticked off at the officiating. One reason the writers like Freddie is he usually stays around to talk long after games, win or lose. But after this game, all he said was:

"In the third period they were stronger—that's where the game was decided. Other than that, I thought Pearl Harbor was over in 1942. That's all."

Then he headed for the elevator. Freddie was one year off on Pearl Harbor, but that's okay: He thought Bryan Lewis, the referee, was off all night.

The fourth game was one I'll never forget. We really wanted to win it so we'd have a 3–1 series lead going back to Philly. We went ahead, 1–0, on Joe Watson's goal, but the Rangers tied it when Bobby Rousseau scored late in the second period. Rousseau's power-play goal was disputed because I thought it hit my glove, then struck the crossbar and came out. The goal judge thought the puck hit my stick, which was over the goal line.

We had to go into overtime. And that's when one of

the worst things that I've ever seen in hockey happened.

The fear of injury is always on our minds, but when the game starts you have to forget it. Some guys are able to do this easier than others. They can be more daring on the ice. I won't say braver because it takes guts just to lace up the skates and go out there.

A guy like Gary Dornhoefer sets up in front of the goalie, as he did against Giacomin in this series, and defies the goalie and defensemen to move him. If they start worrying about Dorny, it takes their attention from the puck. I have to admire a guy like Dorny. He's had a lot of injuries over the years. And he isn't the strongest guy in the world. He even describes himself as "lean, mean, and invisible," but he's a helluva hockey player.

A couple minutes into the overtime Dale Rolfe, the Rangers' defenseman, shot from the left point. I don't think it was a real hard shot, but Barry Ashbee, our defenseman, was partially looking the other way and couldn't move in time. The damn puck hit him just over the right eye. Sometimes when guys get hit and go down, you can tell they are just dazed.

But not this time.

Geez, we could see the blood right away. Barry was covering his face with his hands, and his legs were squirming and we could see he was in terrific pain. He said later it felt like a hot poker had been stuck in his eye.

Frank Lewis, our trainer, was on the ice immediately. "Ashcan" or "Asher," as we call him, was carried off on a stretcher and we tried to get our minds back on the game which, surprisingly, wasn't hard to do. That may sound cruel. Barry had had a helluva season for us (he was voted to the second All-Star team). He played in pain the whole year with a pinched nerve in his neck, but he was always there to do the job.

But here Ashcan was on his way to a hospital after playing what turned out to be his last hockey game and we couldn't allow ourselves to think about him. That's just the way it must be. If you can't concentrate on the game, especially a Stanley Cup game, you'll be in trouble.

We were in trouble a couple minutes later when Rod Gilbert scored the game-winner. A delayed penalty had been called on Dorny, Gilbert got the puck, and Joe Watson was all over him, but he got the shot off. I had moved to the short-side, and the puck went between my legs.

Now it was a best-of-three series, with two of the games at the Spectrum. That home-ice advantage would be very important.

Our bench came through again in the fifth game, which we won 4–1. The Rangers scored first, but a goal by Tom Bladon tied it. Bladon is a young defenseman who was booed a lot by our fans all season. Even though we were going great, I guess people needed somebody to criticize. Tommy wasn't the best defenseman in the league, but he was far from the worst.

After Tommy tied it, we got two goals from MacLeish and one from Simon Nolet. Back to New York and we lost 4–1. Geez, those Rangers could be stubborn. So the series came down to the seventh game. In our building.

The night before the seventh game, we stayed at Stouffers, a hotel near Valley Forge. The guys like the idea of getting together, having a few beers and joking around. It gets the team closer and puts our minds on the game.

When we got up Sunday morning, we had breakfast—many guys only have tea or coffee and toast before an afternoon game—and glanced at the Sunday papers.

Writing in the Philadelphia *Sunday Bulletin,* columnist Jim Barniak began:

> What has been happening to Bernie Parent the past week and a half should only happen to crooked politicians and oil-company executives. It is cruel what they are asking the little guy to endure. Or, to put it in the vernacular of the times, it's downright [unintelligible] inhuman.
>
> Too many times during this current Flyers-Rangers Stanley Cup semi-finals series, Parent has been asked to stand in there and parry a mass of flying hockey pucks that, around the Flyers' goal, look like exploding popcorn kernels. But with reflexes that, to describe, would result in a whole paragraph of superlatives, the guy has survived and the Flyers with him.

What Jim wrote was very complimentary. I had only one complaint: What did he mean by "little guy"?

As we boarded the bus for the Spectrum, the guys were still loose, but as usually happens, everybody quieted down as the thirty-minute trip down the Schuylkill Expressway got started. As the bus gets rolling, most guys either speak quietly to the player sitting next to them or just remain silent.

Sometimes one player will shout some "dig" at another player. The Hound, Bob Kelly, and Rick MacLeish are always needling each other. The Hound heard somebody call Ricky "Hawknose" once so now he'll yell, "Hey, Hawk" and go to cut Ricky up the way only athletes can do.

Ricky usually waits a couple seconds, then tries to shut up the Hound with a quick "shot" but nothing ever keeps the Hound quiet for long. The Hound even picks on Dave Schultz. As we rode in from the St. Louis airport one time, the Hound and Schultzie started on each other. Hound got in the last word with this one:

"Schultzie was standing all night under the arch in downtown St. Louis on our last trip here. He thought it was a McDonald's hamburger place."

When we arrived at the Spectrum, it was warm. By the time we got our gear on, it felt even warmer. We were ready and the crowd was really behind us, but Billy Fairbairn scored first for New York. Ricky tied it for us a minute later, shortly after something happened that might have turned the game in our favor.

It's always hard to say how much fights affect games, but Schultz and Rolfe got into a fight that seemed to take the spark out of the Rangers. I don't think Schultz was getting revenge for Ashbee. Hell, Rolfe felt rotten about what happened to Ashcan. They were roommates at Hershey. With Schultz, Rolfe was just in the wrong place at the wrong time. Schultzie gave him a brutal beating, one of the worst I've seen.

As Schultzie said later, Rolfe just wouldn't go down. And the big thing was, none of the Rangers tried to help Rolfe. They just stood there and let Schultz beat the hell out of him. The Rangers had also let Giacomin alone to handle Dorny the whole series. If someone had set up in the crease like that against me, Moose or Van Impe wouldn't have let them hang around long.

We went ahead 3–1 on goals by Kindrachuk and

Dorny. Steve Vickers scored for New York midway in the third period, but Dorny scored only twelve seconds later, making it 4–2. Stemkowski scored for New York, but we won 4–3. To cap the victory, the Rangers were penalized for having too many men on the ice when they tried to get an extra skater on for Giacomin.

The crowd went wild when the game ended, and so did we. Geez, I was happy and proud. Beating the Rangers, even if we couldn't win on their ice, was a great feeling.

The next day, I read that Brad Park was bitter about the rough way we played. He said the Rangers have a lot of class guys and that he was prouder losing with them than he would be winning with another club. I'm sure he was referring to us.

Well, the series did get out of hand at times, but I noticed that we weren't fighting ourselves and we didn't start all the fights.

Hockey is a rough game.

As Freddie says, if people want pretty skating, they should go to the Ice Capades. To win hockey games, you have to play rough at times. We have class guys, too.

I also noticed that Park said Boston would beat us in the finals. I guess it just wasn't Park's year.

How much chance did we have of whipping Boston? Not much, according to the newspapers. Most of the writers picked the Bruins in five.

Looking back, I'm not even sure we really thought we could beat the Bruins. But when you're playing, things happen so fast that fortunately, you don't have time to consider how you'll do. You have to think you can win or there's no sense playing.

Another advantage of things happening fast, going

from one series to the next, is you don't have a chance to think about how tired you are. We're all in good shape, but we finished the Rangers' series on Sunday and had to play in Boston Tuesday night. The Bruins had been resting for a week after beating Chicago in six games.

Beating Boston was very important to me. A year before, I was in the WHA and had left my team. Now I was trying to help my old team, the underdogs, win the Stanley Cup. A lot was riding on the result.

Usually I try to keep my emotions under control. A goaltender has to stay on a steady emotional level. But the memories I have of games against Boston are ones I'll always cherish.

Maybe what we did, beating the team with the superstars and tradition, will be an inspiration to other teams, no matter what level they're playing. As we proved, it can be done if guys will work together and sacrifice for each other. Whenever I read about teams fighting among themselves, or players criticizing their coach or teammates, I think about our team and the feelings we have for each other.

After we beat Boston, Clarkie had color team photos made up with an inscription that was one of Freddie's blackboard messages: "We will walk together forever." It probably sounds corny to outsiders, but Clarkie is right. The guys on the Philadelphia team that beat Boston will walk together forever.

Going into Boston, we had to be a little worried because we hadn't won in Boston Garden since our first game there in 1967. Since the Bruins had the home-ice advantage, we had to win at least once there to upset them.

Playing in the old Garden brought back memories

for me and, I guess, for the fans who watched me break in as an NHL goalie.

The Garden is in downtown Boston, above North Station. That's right, above a train station. If you've been in any old train stations lately, you know they aren't the cleanest places. As crummy as the Garden may look, though, I give the management credit. They try to keep the station livable. Playing in the Garden is good for the adrenaline because the fans are so close to the ice. Sometimes they are too close, as I found when I was with the Bruins.

The Bruins' dressing room is spacious with carpeting and a nice medical room. The visitor's dressing room isn't so nice. Located down the corridor from the Bruins' room, it is closet-sized. When players have their equipment piled on the floor, there is hardly room to walk.

We didn't get off to the best start in the series, falling behind 2–0 in the first period. I'll bet many Boston fans were sitting there just waiting for us to fold. Of course, we didn't. Kindrachuk and Clarkie got goals to tie it.

With less than a minute to go, Cowboy Bill Flett had a chance to win it when he broke in on Gilles Gilbert, Boston's goalie. But Cowboy's shot hit the post. The Bruins came back, and Moose and Wayne Cashman became tangled up along the boards to my left. We thought the whistle should have blown, but Ken Hodge got to the puck and passed it to Orr. Orr let go a thirty-five-footer that beat me with twenty-two seconds left in regulation time.

Sure I felt bad, but I also knew that getting beat by Bobby Orr isn't a disgrace. And I kept thinking that they **needed** that goal to keep us from taking them into overtime. When we won the next game in overtime to crack our Boston jinx, people said it was the turning point in the series. Well, I think the first game showed us the Bruins were beatable. Now we just had to do it.

We were trailing 2–1 in the second game with under a minute to play in the third period when Moose Dupont drilled one past Gilbert to tie it. Right away Dupont went into his "Moose Shuffle" where he runs on his skates and waves his arms. Other teams probably think Moose is acting like a hot dog, but what the hell, it shows he's enjoying the game.

Freddie tells a story about coaching in the minor leagues against a guy who did a dance after every goal is scored. Finally Freddie couldn't stand it anymore, and when the guy went into his dance, Freddie sent out someone who dropped the dancer. Freddie says it was the guy's last dance.

Tying the Bruins was one thing; beating them in the Garden was another. Moose said later that after his goal he looked at the Boston bench and they all had their heads down. Moose said he thought then that we would win it.

The Bruins best scoring chance in the overtime was a Johnny Bucyk shot. Bucyk has been around a long time, over twenty years in the league, so he knows all the tricks, but I've always felt in an overtime you have to be aggressive. A team must challenge and so must the goaltender.

Bucyk came in from my right. He was really motoring, so I moved out to the edge of the crease and waited for his move. He faked on the short side, then shot, but I stopped it with my chest.

About two minutes later Clarkie won it for us. Schultz

was on for his first shift in overtime. He dug the puck out of the corner to Gilbert's right and passed to Flett in the slot. Cowboy fed the puck to Clarkie, who had played a helluva game. Clarkie shot, the rebound came back to him, and he put it over Gilbert and Terry O'Reilly, who had dived into the crease trying to prevent the score.

When the red light went on, Clarkie looked like John Havlicek, jumping toward the Garden roof. We all mobbed Clarkie, then headed to the dressing room and the flight home.

Freddie admitted after the game he had had doubts about us winning the cup. However, now he knew we could do it. So did I. Boston had to be worried.

Back at the Sprectrum we won 4–1. Bladon tied it and Crispie put us ahead to stay. There's that depth again, everybody contributing. The win was costly, though. Dorny was checked cleanly by Don Marcotte and came out with a separated shoulder. Dorny was through for the series. We all felt bad because Dorny has broken a lot of bones for the Flyers and wanted to be on a Stanley Cup winner, but it was just like Ashbee's injury: we had to keep going.

The next game at the Spectrum was critical. If we could win, we'd go back to Boston with a 3–1 edge. The Bruins would have to win three straight for the cup, and the way we were playing that wasn't likely.

Billy Barber scored the big goal for us, a wrist shot from the left side that put us ahead 3–2 late in the third period. Orr said it was the best wrist shot he had seen all season. Moose scored a few minutes later and we had a 4–2 win. The cup was really close.

The Bruins didn't go down easy. When the score was 2–2, they had a great chance to score. I was down after reaching for the rebound of a Bucyk shot. I couldn't get back up and Bobby Schmautz had the whole net to shoot at. But he missed from ten feet. All I could think was Bernie, you're a lucky so-and-so.

I wish I could say we didn't win the next game because we wanted to clinch the series before our fans, but that wouldn't be true. You don't toy with the Bruins. Give them too many chances and their names will be on the cup, not yours. Orr got two goals in the second period to break a 1–1 tie and the Bruins won 5–1.

Probably what most people remember about the game is the penalties. It seemed like the game went on forever (game time was three hours, twenty-three minutes). In the first minute Schultzie and Carol Vadnais got into a fight. Before the night was over, Schultzie took on Cashman and practically the whole Boston team. Dave Newell called forty-three penalties, a Stanley Cup game record.

Before the sixth game, Bep Guidolin, Boston's coach, said the Bruins hadn't played a good game in Philly, so in the series Guidolin insisted that the Bruins were due. He was right. They did play a helluva game, but we were just a little better.

Guidolin is quite a character. He was the youngest player ever in the NHL turning pro with the Bruins when he was sixteen. Later, he coached Orr at Oshawa and was promoted to the Bruins after coaching their American League farm team.

Guidolin can be a gruff guy, but he also has a sense of humor. He broke us up at the Stanley Cup luncheon held at the Spectrum before game three. None of the Bruins showed up while about a half dozen Flyers were there. When it was Bep's turn to speak, he said:

"It's nice to see the Philadelphia players here. It's nice to see my players at the racetrack."

The Bruins were staying in Cherry Hill, New Jersey, near Garden State Racetrack.

For the sixth game the club brought in Kate Smith. This time most people expected her.

Everybody got another lift when Barry Ashbee walked in to Mr. Snider's super box before the first face-off. Some players had spoken to Ashcan or visited him in the hospital, but this was the first time he could attend a game since his eye injury.

To show how great our fans are, when the people in front of the super boxes spotted Asher they gave him a standing ovation. Everybody in the building caught on and all 17,007 were on their feet applauding.

Later, when I thought about that incident, it was another example of the warm feeling our fans have for the team. Say what you want about sports, when a team can make people react the way they did toward Asher, we're doing something right.

The game's only goal was scored in the first period when Rick MacLeish skated in front of Gilbert and deflected a power-play shot by Moose Dupont. Gilbert never had a chance.

The Bruins kept coming at us. Ken Hodge had their last good chance with about three minutes to go, a slapshot from about thirty feet that I deflected with my stick. When Orr went off for holding Clarkie with 2:22 to play, we felt the cup was almost ours.

Having Orr out of Boston's lineup is like taking O. J. Simpson away from the Buffalo Bills. All through the series our plan had been to bother Bobby, tire him out. We'd try to bump him after he gave up the puck, anything to slow him down and prevent him from skating. The average playing time for a hockey player is twenty to twenty-five minutes a game. Orr always plays more than that, and in this game, somebody said he was on the ice for almost forty minutes.

When time ran out, the Spectrum just exploded with noise. So many people rushed onto the ice that we could just about move. Somehow they got Clarence Campbell and the Stanley Cup on the ice. Clarkie and I were supposed to carry the cup around the ice, but it was impossible.

The dressing room was a madhouse with people and cameras. Players were hugging and slapping each other on the back. Some players threw Mr. Snider in the shower, after we had poured champagne over him.

One scene I remember from the celebration was Ashbee, wearing dark glasses and standing along the wall between the showers and the medical room. He told people that he doesn't cry much, but he was in tears the last couple minutes of the game. Maybe if I had time in those final minutes I would have cried, too. Tears of joy.

When I had the chance, I moved into the medical room. Clarkie, Ross Lonsberry, and a couple other players were there, too. We just had to get away from the people and microphones and be by ourselves.

Favell was in the medical room, too. He was playing for the new Philadelphia Wings lacrosse team, which was opening its season that night at the Spectrum. He had worked out with us the day before. When Freddie saw him, he smiled and asked Favvy to put on the pads "to give our players confidence."

Favvy shook hands with me and seemed happy for all of us. Even though he was with Toronto now, I knew he still felt like part of us.

"It's funny, sitting here and watching all this," Favvy said. "A year after I'm traded and I still feel close to these guys."

Usually the medical room is off limits to the press, but this was an exception. I was lying on a trainer's table, smoking a cigarette and drinking a beer. That's when I started talking about how winning the cup felt.

I remembered first thinking about winning the cup back in Montreal when I was five or six years old. I saw the Canadiens and Chicago play a game on TV until almost two o'clock in the morning. It was such a tremendous thing, and I wondered what the feeling would be to play for the cup.

At this time, it was too soon to know how it really felt. I looked over to the other table where Clarkie was talking with writers. It was so hot that I noticed Clarkie was pouring beer on himself. I thought again about what an example Clarkie was for us—always working, no matter how tired he was. Work. That's how we won, by just working harder than the other teams.

Just before our wives came into the room—did that ever happen before?—I thought about winning the cup and I knew that even a million dollars couldn't buy the feeling we had now.

FREDDIE
SHERO

The first thing you learn when you turn pro is to carry a church key.

Topping the list of people I have met in hockey is Fred Shero.

Freddie and I don't live far apart in Cherry Hill, New Jersey. I often drive with him to the Philadelphia International Airport. You'd think that after all the time we spend together I'd feel I know Freddie better. Well, I don't. I'm sure hardly anybody really knows Freddie. I'm also sure he wants it that way.

Part of his success is not getting involved with people. Freddie has no friends and he has no enemies. Don't get me wrong: Freddie is easy to get along with. He can joke with the players, even kid us about the amount of money we get. He sincerely wants to make his players better men, but he only goes so far. He opens the doors, but it's up to us to walk through them.

When Billy Clement was traded to Washington after last season, he told the writers: "I've cursed him [Shero] when I thought I should be playing. But I still respect him. He earned my respect, he didn't demand it. He has that intangible ability to keep so many people happy without getting involved. He's a very compassionate man who loves everybody he coaches."

Those sayings Freddie writes on the blackboard in our dressing room have become kind of famous.

You might think professional hockey players would laugh at anyone who tried psyching them up with blackboard messages. That kind of rah-rah went out in high school. Well, we've learned to think about Freddie's messages because the man has become so successful. People probably laughed at the person

174

who invented Frisbees, but when they started selling by the millions the laughter stopped.

It's the same thing with Freddie's blackboard sayings and notes that he hands you. He'll write on the board clichés like "When the going gets tough, the tough get going," but most of his inspirational sayings aren't as well known. Things like "History has proven that, in the majority of cases, a man who fails to achieve an attainable goal cannot justly blame it on circumstance."

Freddie will walk over to you while you're sitting at your locker, say, "Here, I have something for you," and walk away. You don't throw the note in the trash. You think, "Hey, this might mean something." Maybe I'm doing something wrong as a man. So you read it and think about it.

When Cowboy Flett was in a slump during the play-offs when we won our first Stanley Cup, Freddie gave Cowboy an envelope that contained, in part, this message: "It is not the critic who counts . . . the man who points out where the strong man stumbled . . . where the doer of deeds could have done better. The credit belongs to the man who is actually in the arena, whose face is marred with dust and sweat and blood . . . who strives valiantly . . . who errs and comes up short and tries again. . . ."

Cowboy taped the note inside his locker.

A year later, after the Flyers traded to get Reggie Leach from California, Freddie called Reggie in for a talk after purposely failing to keep appointments. That's another of Freddie's gimmicks. He'll keep breaking appointments with players to make them think about why he wants to see them.

When they finally met in the coach's office at the Spectrum, Freddie asked what Reggie wanted out of life.

"I want to win," Reggie said.

When Reggie was asked if he had ever been on a winner, he answered, "Yes, with Flin Flon." (That's where Reggie and Clarkie were junior teammates.)

"That's small potatoes," Freddie said.

Reggie had never been with a professional championship team.

He was the third player chosen in the 1970 amateur draft, after Gil Perreault and Dale Tallon. Boston had no room for him, however, and in February 1972 he was traded to California with two others for Carol Vadnais. Reggie found no motivation in the losing atmosphere in California.

"What I'm trying to tell you," Freddie said, "is that it takes more than talent to win championships in the big leagues. You have to go beyond yourself."

In his first season as a Flyer, Reggie scored forty-five goals, then added eight more in the play-offs.

Before our fourth semifinal game against the Islanders last season, Freddie gave this mimeographed message to the players: "No horse ever gets anywhere until it's harnessed; no system or gas ever drives anything until it's confined; no Niagara ever turns into light and power until its tunneled."

As Jack Chevalier of the Philadelphia *Evening Bulletin* wrote, Freddie meant "the Flyers can sweep the Islanders if they harness their exuberance with discipline."

While the players have great respect for Freddie's messages they don't hesitate to "comment" on them.

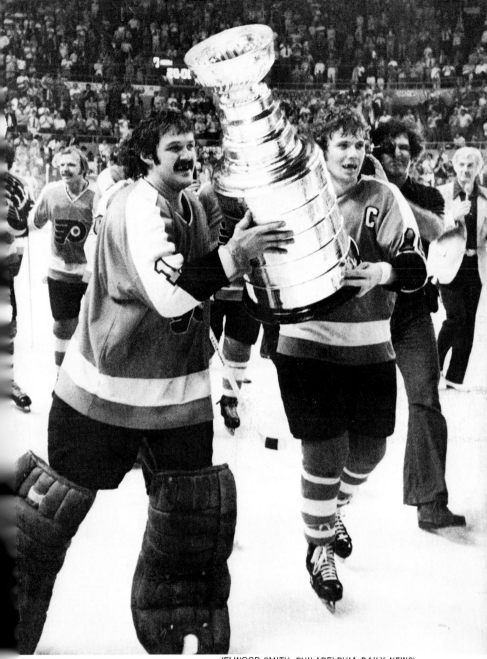

Clarkie and I take the Stanley Cup for a little ride while some of the gang look on. That was the greatest feeling I have ever had.

(BERNIE MOSER FLYER'S PHOTO)

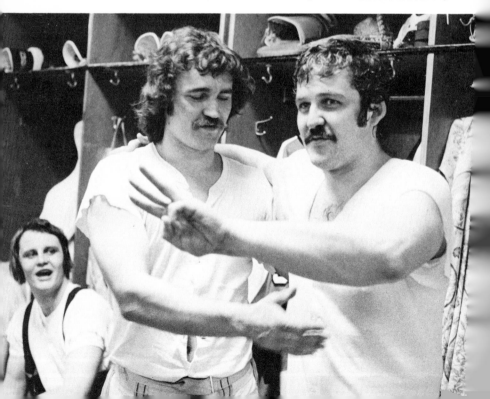

Kate Smith is the only dry one as she congratulated Ed Snider and Bobby Clarke.

Left above: The celebration. Trainer Frank Lewis, Bobby Taylor, Dorny and I do a little whooping it up.

Left below: I may have been predicting three cups in a row here. We all get carried away now and then, but we'll be trying, that's for sure. Bill Barber and Rick MacLeish agree — I hope.

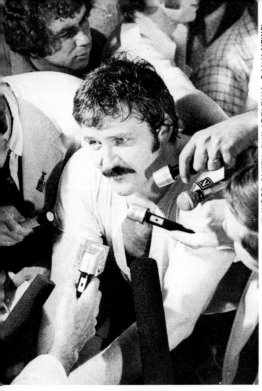

(ELWOOD SMITH, PHILADELPHIA *DAILY NEWS*)

Things have calmed down a little here as I relax and try to answer some questions after our final victory over Buffalo.

Another question. It's all part of winning. If they didn't ask any, then I would really get worried.

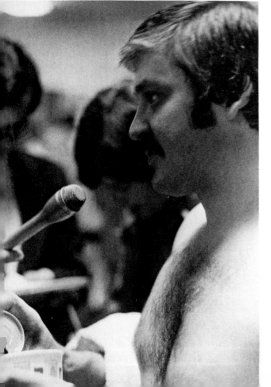

This crowd in front of City Hall greeted us after our victory in Buffalo. I've never experienced anything like the Flyer fans — they're number one.

(BERNIE MOSER FLYER'S PHOTO

Mayor Frank Rizzo presents me with one of the trophies that each player received from the City of Philadelphia.

Left above: After our first Stanley Cup we had quite a celebration too. I flash a double victory sign as my wife Carol, Mayor Rizzo behind me, and Kate Smith provide the singing.

Left below: Kate Smith and Mike Douglas joined the South Philadelphia String Band in giving us a rousing welcome on television.

Clarkie and I ham it up for the photographers.

We had a couple of victory parties after the championship. Joe and Mary Ann Watson, Ed and Diane Van Impe, Rick MacLeish, Carol and I all had a good time at this one.

One day Freddie put this thought on the dressing room blackboard:

> Four things come not back:
> —the spoken word
> —the sped arrow
> —the past life
> —the neglected opportunity

After the "sped arrow," somebody wrote "For the Chief" (Bobby Taylor, our backup goalie).

After we read, "The greatest oak was once a little nut that held its ground" somebody added, "Kelly, take note."

Freddie really depends on his blackboard. He once threatened to move the team out of our hotel in Boston because the hotel couldn't provide him with a blackboard.

People often think of hockey players as dumb jocks because guys would never finish school. It's changing now. We're getting more college players in the league. And even those of us who didn't go to college are interested in new things.

Making good money and having opportunities to travel open new areas. If a man doesn't take advantage of all this, then he is a dummy.

"I'll admit my first exposure to Freddie had me wondering. When I was traded to Toronto, Vic Stasiuk was still coaching the Flyers, so I didn't meet Freddie until he had been with the Flyers two years. The contrast between Freddie and Vic was as clear as the difference between Walter Alston and Billy Martin.

Vic had been a big, tough NHL player who had moved up as a coach in the Philadelphia organization.

Vic's biggest problem was he could never adjust to the modern hockey player. Vic was a shouter. He'd yell behind the bench, in the dressing room, and at practice. You might even be talking with Vic in an airport or hotel lobby when suddenly he would grab you and demonstrate how to check or shoot. Most current players don't live hockey twenty-four hours a day, but Vic could never understand that.

To illustrate how wrapped up in hockey Vic was, one night after a game he woke me up by calling me at home at three or four o'clock in the morning. We had lost 2–1 and Vic had gone home, where he watched the video tapes.

"Bernie," Vic said over the phone, "remember their winning goal? Well, next time on a shot like that come out [from the cage] but don't come out."

Then all I heard was "click" and Vic had hung up. I was half groggy, so I couldn't think too much about what he said.

A few days later, we were on the bus to the hotel in Chicago. By then I had told the guys about Vic's middle-of-the-night telephone call, so as the bus neared the hotel, I stood up, turned to the team, and said: "Wait a minute. When the bus pulls up to the hotel, get off, but don't get off."

The guys laughed like crazy, but Vic didn't crack a smile. I don't think he remembered talking to me on the phone.

Once, when things were going bad for us, Vic banned speaking French on the ice or in the dressing room. This didn't go over too well with Simon Nolet, Guy Gendron, Andy Lacroix, or myself. Vic meant well, trying to stress a team feeling with everyone speaking the same language, but the way he went about it ticked us off. He should have asked us if we would mind not speaking French around the other players.

People tell me Vic is a good guy, but he never let the players see that side of him. Even in later NHL coaching jobs with California and Vancouver he didn't change. I understand he is back in Lethbridge, Alberta, working on his farm and coaching a junior team. Maybe he'll be happy there. I hope so.

By the time I returned to the Flyers Freddie had been with the club for two years. His first season had an awful ending when Gerry Meehan scored for Buffalo with four seconds left to knock the club out of the play-offs. The next season they surprised a lot of people by reaching the Stanley Cup semifinals before losing to Montreal.

Freddie's reputation was just starting to spread. I had heard stories about him, but I wanted to see for myself.

At first, I thought the exercises and things he had us doing were the kind you give to a peewee or bantam players. Cripes, you feel a little funny holding hands with another player, or sitting on a chair while a teammate pushes you up and down the ice. But then I realized they all had a purpose. Even professionals need reminders about fundamentals, and the conditioning is always good. Blend all these drills with a professional's experience and you have a good, healthy team. In my two years back with the Flyers, we've had very few pulled-muscle injuries. I think Freddie's program, combined with the Apollo exercises we do, are responsible for the small number of injuries.

187

Freddie is always looking to be one step ahead of the times.

He's constantly reading, and somewhere, somehow, Freddie read about the special exercise program that the Apollo astronauts were following.

Next thing the Flyers knew, Freddie had the guys training for outer space.

The exercise program was first demonstrated to Clarkie and Gary Dornhoefer during the spring of 1973. Both Clarkie and Dorny started using it almost immediately. They continued with it right through the Flyers' successful spring season when the club reached the semifinals before being eliminated by the Canadiens.

By the time I rejoined the club, Freddie had decided that the entire team was going to be pulling on the ropes a la Wally Schirra and James Lovell.

During our last two Stanley Cup–winning season, Carmen Martucci, whom I kiddingly refer to as "the Wild Italian," and Dr. John Glassey, Apollo training consultants, have been teaching us isokinetics.

Now, isokinetics is a pretty fancy-sounding word, but what it basically boils down to is a method designed to increase flexibility, endurance, and strength—three major ingredients for any outstanding athletic team.

The only thing that bothers me about the Apollo program is now that I'm all prepared to fly to the moon, I don't really feel like going.

With my luck, there wouldn't be any caribou to hunt and the first moonman I met would probably have a slapshot five times as fast as Bobby Hull.

Another thing with Freddie is he's always the same, whether it's with Clarkie or me or Frank Lewis, our trainer. Freddie says what he has to and moves on. I don't think I've ever seen him in the dressing room after a game, win or lose.

Everybody kids Freddie about being the "Phantom." You'll be standing outside a hotel and suddenly Freddie's right there. A few minutes later you look away for a second, and when you turn back, he's gone.

The way Freddie keeps practices interesting is another of his strengths. Cripes, some days he'll say a couple things at the start of practice, then turn it over to Mike and Barry and disappear.

There's a story about how unpredictable Freddie is that really sums him up.

The team was on a bus after a game and Joe Watson discovered the beer cans were the old kind, without the pull-tops. Joe started yelling, "What are we gonna do?" People back in Joe's hometown of Smithers, B.C., could probably hear him.

While Joe was yelling, Freddie got up from his seat in front of the bus, walked down the aisle, reached in his pocket, and handed Joe a church key.

"The first thing you learn when you turn pro is to carry a church key," Freddie said, and walked back to his seat. The guys broke up.

Freddie has a story that tops almost every current development in hockey. He'll tell how his team in St. Paul once played a game until three o'clock in the morning. Or how when his team was in the play-offs in Houston he told them to stay out of the sun. The best place for them, he said, was an air-conditioned bar. And this was the day of a big game!

Freddie can never sleep late. I think he has trouble sleeping mainly because of his bad back, but he says:

"I get up early deliberately. Then I can look at the people going to work. I can think how lucky I am. I can go back to sleep, call off practice, do anything I want."

Freddie never hesitated when the idea of hiring Mike Nykoluk as modern hockey's first full-time assistant coach was presented.

"Having two coaches will keep the players busy," Freddie said. "Most coaches don't want to admit they need help. They're afraid for their jobs."

If Freddie is ever completely happy, he doesn't show it. He'll say he prefers being miserable because you can't know joy until you've known misery.

When we were watching the color Stanley Cup action film during training camp, I asked Freddie if he enjoyed reliving our victory.

"No, I don't watch fil-lums to enjoy them. I watch them to learn and you can't learn anything from a fil-lum like that."

One of the few times Philadelphia management was angry with its eccentric coach was when the story broke that he was considering a WHA job. The Flyers finally offered Freddie a better contract, and when he showed up for the press conference at the Spectrum, he acted as if nothing had happened. Then he stopped the show with this tale:

"When I was in Moscow this summer, my wife and I went to pray. I prayed I would never have to leave Philadelphia."

Here Keith Allen and Mr. Snider had been in Philly worrying about losing their coach and Freddie was in Moscow praying he would never leave. How can you figure the man?

Freddie's "meetings" fit right in with all the stories

about him. Sure, sometimes they are serious and we go over what we'll do in the game. But then there are "meetings" like the one in Atlanta last season.

All the players and coaches were in Freddie's Marriott Hotel suite. Freddie walks in, takes out a newspaper clipping about a Russian family that had blasted the style of living in America and returned to Russia.

"These people must enjoy misery," Freddie said and left the room. End of meeting. We all laughed, but we also thought Freddie was giving us something to think about—we are all fortunate to be living like we are.

There is only one Freddie Shero. That's one reason I gave him the Javelin car I won from *Sport Magazine* after the 1974 Stanley Cup play-offs. When I gave Freddie the keys, he said, "I've always said you have to be a little goofy to be a coach. But now I think my players are a little crazy, too."

Freddie said my wife would kill me if I gave him the car, but I laughed and said, "Ah, she's already tried it a couple times."

I just thought Freddie deserved a gift like that. He took us to the cup. Sure we had a good team, but he's the one who harnessed us and kept us going.

Freddie didn't drive the car until the end of the 1974–75 season. If we beat Atlanta in the final game, we would have the home-ice advantage in the play-offs. Freddie said he wanted to ensure a win, so he drove the "Green Hornet" to the Spectrum and we won. Sometimes Freddie is like that song, "When You're Hot, You're Hot."

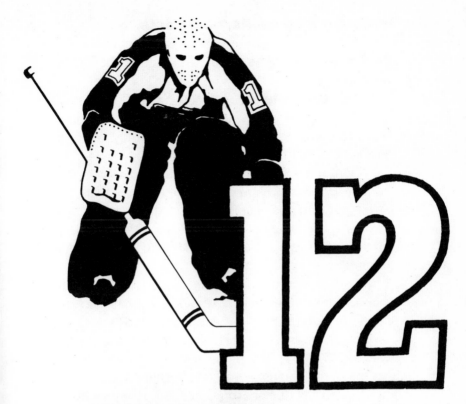

HOCKEY STARS AND MY ALL-TIME ALL-STAR TEAM

Players run on hearts, not motors.

Ed Snider. The Flyers have made some good decisions in their front office.

Mr. Snider is different from most owners because he gets involved. Many owners don't really care much about the players. The team is either a toy or just a business to them.

When Bernie Brown took over the Blazers from Jim Cooper, Brown said he was going to run the team like his big trucking business. Cripes, you just can't do that. Players run on hearts, not motors. If a player isn't performing up to par, you can't send him to the shop for a tune-up.

Some owners don't even know the players. When you meet them, they'll say, "What's your name?" I hear Charlie Finley was that way when he owned the California Golden Seals. Geez, if I'm the boss of a company, I want to know the employees and what makes them tick.

Snider really seems to care about his players. I think he's basically a businessman, but he's very emotional about the team. He wants us to win—after all, it is a big business. If we lost, I wouldn't expect him to say, "Tough luck, fellas." But if you produce for him, he'll do almost anything for you.

The Flyers once had a player who had piled up debts across the United States and Canada. His motto must have been "Spend now, I'll pay you if you can catch me." He was always borrowing money.

Well, Snider thought the player could help the Flyers, so he worked out a plan to pay off all the debts. I don't know how the plan turned out—the player isn't in the NHL anymore—but just the fact that Snider tried to help him impresses me.

One reason the Flyers are on top is that when the WHA first tried to sign NHL players, Snider went out of his way to keep his club together. I know some fans complain that they are paying for the club's success through higher ticket prices, but I don't think most people mind paying when the club wins. They'll pay for quality.

Mr. Snider is also good about footing the bill for anything that gets the team together. Clarkie has never been turned down when he has gone to Mr. Snider and asked him to arrange a get-together.

When seven of our players had to stand trial for fighting with the fans in Pacific Coliseum in Vancouver a couple years ago, they were supposed to be there three days. Instead they were there for seven days and Mr. Snider paid for all their expenses.

Keith Allen. For a while after I was traded to Toronto, Keith wasn't my favorite person. It wasn't anything personal, but he's the one who had traded me. When that happens, you don't feel like taking the man responsible out to dinner. Still Keith has always been a classy person. I don't remember much about him as a coach, but as a manager you have to respect him for all the moves he has made. His trades have brought Rick MacLeish, Reggie Leach, Ross Lonsberry, Moose Dupont, Terry Crisp, Ted Harris, and Wayne Stephenson to Philly. And it was Keith who made the deal to bring me back. Keith is good about staying away and letting Freddie run the team. They confer a lot, but Freddie is in charge of the daily operation of the team. On **many**

195

teams, the manager or owner is always giving the coach orders.

Marcel Pelletier. He's a great help to me. I'm probably closer to him than anyone in the organization. Marcel is a former goaltender, so he is able to spot my mistakes. He'll notice if I'm backing into the net too much, or going behind the net to stop the puck too often. Sometimes after practice, we'll have a sandwich and talk over my mistakes. Marcel's title is player personnel director. He keeps an eye on the farm teams and scouts the NHL, WHA, and minor leagues. He and Freddie have known each other a long time and work well together.

All our guys are great, but I think a couple rate special mention.

Bobby Clarke. There is probably no one else like Clarkie in hockey. He's an inspiration to us. Hockey players like to think they are tough-skinned, but when we see how Clarkie works, it makes us all play harder. He doesn't like people mentioning his diabetes, but damn, we see him in the dressing room between periods taking off his skates because his feet get sore. When we think about him going through problems like that every day, we all want to work our tails off. Clarkie reminds me a lot of Jean Béliveau when he was Montreal's captain. Both are very quiet, but they are great leaders. Clarkie's judgment is amazing. He always seems to know the right thing to say. And he'll give you the shirt off his back. He told me if we beat Buffalo and won the Stanley Cup, he'd buy me a Jeep. We used that Renegade Jeep all summer around Wildwood. When Dougie was traded to Toronto to complete the deal that brought me back to Philly, Clarkie showed up at the summer press conference at the Spectrum and tried making it easier for Dougie to accept the news.

Dave Schultz. Schultz plays a much bigger role on our team than many people think. He's like John Ferguson was for Montreal. Having Schultzie around is like having extra security. It's like going on a camping trip when bears are around and having someone there who makes you feel safe. None of us is the tiptoe type. We can all take care of ourselves, but a guy like Schultzie keeps things in order. Schultzie is willing to fight, home or away. And if he loses he comes right back. I don't think he worries about losing fights. Some Islanders' people got excited in the play-offs when Dave was losing to Clark Gillies and Moose went in to help Dave. Maybe those people forget that it was the third period and Dave was tired. Anyway, Gillies is a big guy, 6'3", 220 pounds, and losing a fight to him is no disgrace. People might be surprised to learn that Dave doesn't spend the day of a game growling at old ladies in hotel lobbies. He's a very quiet guy off the ice. He just knew that to make the NHL he'd have to play tough. I'm told that for a while he was pretty bad as a hockey player, but he has worked hard to improve himself. I'm glad he's on our side.

Bob Kelly. When Kelly came to us as a rookie out of junior hockey, he was given the nickname Mad Dog for his reckless style. Now we call him Hound or Mutt.

The Hound has taken a lot of kidding, but he has learned to give it back pretty good. He and Gene Hart, our announcer, are always joking. Kelly tells Gene, who weighs about 270 pounds, that his pants are flared at the wrong end.

On his first trip to L.A. with us, some guys convinced

the Hound a store was having a sale on snow tires. If it ever snows in L.A., Phyllis Diller will win a beauty contest.

During his rookie year, some of us arranged to take the Hound snipe hunting around Philly. We even set it up so the cops would arrest us for hunting snipe out of season. When they took us off to jail, Kelly was scared as hell. And the rest of us could hardly keep from laughing.

Another time, the Hound was looking for a new Corvette. So he went to a Korvette's department store expecting to find a big selection of shiny new cars.

Our appearances in the last two Stanley Cup finals have made us near experts on Boston and Buffalo players. Some of the top players and my impressions:

Phil Esposito. Some say he's a garbageman the way he scores all his points. Well, if every garbageman earned his kind of money, they'd be in good shape. In my time he's the best goal scorer I've seen. The reasons are he's always in good position and he has great balance. Even if he gets knocked off balance, which only happens if the other team dresses a Mack truck as a defenseman, he still gets his shot off. Our fans and others around the league get mad at Esposito when he complains to the referees about their not calling enough penalties. The fans think he cries too much. Well, the guy takes a helluva beating in front of the net, so I can't blame him for griping. Another thing you hear is that for someone his size (6'1", 210) he lets others do his fighting. Again, I can't criticize him. Every team has guys to do different things. If Esposito fought every time somebody gave him a shot, he'd be in the penalty box all night. The Bruins want him on the ice—to make goalies like myself miserable.

Bobby Orr. Sorry, but I can't add anything new about Orr. He is just the most talented, all-around hockey player I have ever seen. Some, like Freddie Shero, say he is too offensive-minded. With his ability he'd be foolish not to spark Boston's offense. And don't let anybody tell you he is only average defensively. He is one of the best.

The French Connection Line. All three—Richard Martin, Gil Perreault, and René Robert—are enough to give goalies gray hair. In my case, make that more gray hair. Martin's shot is the best I have seen since Bobby Hull. One time after he shot, our guys heard me mumbling. Maybe they thought I had finally cracked. When they skated over, all I said was "Geez, that kid can really shoot the puck."

Perreault can shoot, skate, and pass. From a fan's view it must be tough deciding whether Perreault or Orr is the more exciting player. All I know is I wish they would both retire. Wait, I don't mean that. The game needs both of them.

Robert is a great example of a guy who kept working even though he had setbacks. He bounced around the Toronto system for a couple years, then Pittsburgh got him and gave up on him. Cripes, Pittsburgh traded him to Buffalo for Eddie Shack. At the time it looked like a nothing deal, but now Buffalo has a helluva player. They tell me Robert has become a real leader for the Sabres.

I'm not mentioning other NHL goalies because I honestly don't notice them much during games. I'm too busy concentrating on the shooters.

All I'll say about goaltenders is there is no way you can rate them. There isn't much difference among NHL goalies.

Here's the best example:

When Jacques Plante played for Montreal, he won five Vezina Trophies in a row. When he was traded to New York, he had the same ability, but he was with a poor team, so he couldn't perform. Gump Worsley played for New York and had never won anything in his life, but he went to Montreal and won the Vezina. I know it's a cliché, but it's true: Being in the right place at the right time often makes a goalie look great.

People have asked who would be on my all-time NHL All-Star team. From ones I've played against here are my selections:

Goalie: Jacques Plante. Maybe I'm prejudiced toward him, but he was a great player, a pioneer, and he helped me.

Defense: Bobby Orr and J. C. Tremblay. Orr would be the best at any position he played. Tremblay didn't have Orr's speed, but his anticipation was great and he handled the puck like a master.

Center: Bobby Clarke. For all-around play, not just scoring goals. Besides, if he ever writes a book, maybe he'll pick me.

Left wing: Bobby Hull. For his speed, shot, and devotion to helping hockey. The first year of the WHA he worked his tail off signing autographs and making public appearances even on game days. Once, when Bobby was with Chicago, the writers asked me what I do when Hull shoots. I just smiled and said, "Try not to get hurt."

Right wing: Gordie Howe. He was so strong he

could beat you in a lot of ways. Anybody who can play until he is forty-seven years old and score 786 NHL goals is an automatic All-Star. When I'm forty-seven I'll probably be captain on a fishing boat, smoking a cigar, sipping a beer, and hollering, "Hard to starboard!"

I've played on teams with many funny guys, so picking an All-Flake team might be fun.

Goalie: Gerry Cheevers and Doug Favell. Both never seem to let anything worry them. When the Bruins would play Chicago, Cheevers would tell the team to make sure they stood in front of him so he wouldn't get hurt when Bobby Hull shot. Another time, when Hap Emms was the Bruins' G.M., they lost 10–2. Emms asked Cheevers what happened and he said, "Roses are red. Violets are blue. They got ten. And we only got two."

Favvy was joking around. I guess the most familiar story about him was the time in our first season in Philly when he walked into the dressing room eating pizza and drinking a Coke. He thought I was playing, but I had the flu, so he had to play. The crazy thing was he won to clinch the first-half Vezina award for us. One of the times Favvy was in Freddie's doghouse was during the lettuce boycott in California led by César Chavéz. When a writer asked Dougie if he felt he was being boycotted, Dougie replied, "What do I look like, a head of lettuce?" When the club returned home, Andy Walker, a Spectrum carpenter, had put a head of lettuce in Dougie's locker.

Defense: Larry Zeidel and Joe Watson. "Rock" Zeidel was really something. After one game where he dressed but didn't play he was still walking around the dressing room forty-five minutes later. When I asked what he was doing, the Rock said, "Since I didn't play tonight I'm working mentally." When the Rock was hired as a Flyers' announcer, they tell me he used to "get up" for games by wrestling with Pat Shetler, the NHL linesman who was his partner for a while. Joe Watson makes the team because he always breaks us up by being himself. Loud. Take Joe hunting and he'd scare a mountain.

Center: Forbes Kennedy. Forbesy was afraid of mice. Guys used to put mice in his skates and scare him stiff. He always had a funny story for us.

Left wing: Eddie Shack. After their stick fight this is the only team Shack and Larry Zeidel would be on together. One time Shack was being chased around the ice by four or five guys, so he jumped behind his own bench and told his teammates, "Go get 'em for me."

Right wing: Simon Nolet. Simon isn't really a flake. He's just a friendly, honest guy whom everybody likes to have around, on and off the ice. He hated leaving the Flyers, but Kansas City made him captain and he led them in scoring.

People have urged me to name the "most overrated" players in hockey. No thanks, the game is tough enough. Besides, who am I to criticize? However, it does bother me to see guys getting good money who don't perform. There are some in the league who just loaf on the ice. They know who they are, and so do their fans.

MY FAMILY

Hockey players are just cuddly teddy bears.

My first couple years in Philly I enjoyed myself as any normal young red-blooded French-Canadian man would.

Language was still a problem—I didn't quite sound like Sir Laurence Olivier when I spoke English—but if I stayed with the other players I got along okay.

Carol and I met at a Christmas party in 1967. She was with another guy and I was with another girl, but we seemed to hit it off and started dating. She told me later that she hadn't been interested in hockey until a girl friend suggested they go to a Jersey Devils' game. The Devils played in the old Eastern League at what was then the Cherry Hill Arena, now called the Centrum. Then Carol went on dates to a couple Flyers' games.

Carol was also living right around the corner from me in the Barrington Manor Apartments, so we saw a lot of each other. I don't think her family was too wild about her dating a hockey player. Before they met me, they thought all hockey players were animals, brutes who had stomped down from the Canadian wilderness devouring villages on the way. After meeting me, they discovered hockey players are just cuddly teddy bears (believe that and I'll offer you a good deal on the Montreal subway system).

Carol kept after me to meet her parents, but I kept postponing it. It's strange: I usually enjoy myself around people, but I'm often reluctant to meet new people. Maybe I'm just shy, or maybe I still don't feel completely comfortable around people who speak English, or maybe I just prefer being with people I know.

Anyway, I finally agreed to meet Carol's parents. But I told her, "We'll just go over, eat, and leave."

On the way to the Wilsons' Haddonfield, New Jersey, home, I was really nervous and almost turned around a couple times. But when we got there and I met "Big Dick," we all hit it off. We had a great time and didn't leave until three o'clock in the morning.

I guess I put Carol through a tough time before we got engaged. I went back to Montreal that summer and told her I would write, but never did. When I came back for our second season in Philly we started dating, and around Christmas I proposed. I guess that's what you would call it. I sure as hell didn't follow the "Cary Grant Guide to Romancing Women."

We were out somewhere and I asked Carol:

"Would you marry me if I asked you to?"

She didn't know if I was fooling around or what, so she said something like "Yeah, I guess I would."

Then I said, "Well, would you?"

I was really in control, eh? It's a good thing I was sitting down. If I were standing, my "Jell-O knees" wouldn't have held me.

Carol said yes and the next day we bought a diamond. She didn't pick out a big diamond. Hell, I was in such a fog she could have picked a rock the size of the ones Richard Burton gives Elizabeth Taylor and I wouldn't have known the difference.

We planned a big July wedding. All the invitations were out and everything was set when I came down to Jersey a week before the wedding and said, "It's off. I can't go through with it. I don't think I'm ready to get married."

Talk about cold feet! I had chills all through my body.

I had to get away, so some friends and I went hunting in the Canadian Rockies. I had time to think there and finally decided, what the hell, do it! Maybe I was too young (I was twenty-three), but I loved the girl.

When we got back to Montreal, I called Carol and told her the Flyers would be training in Hershey, Pennsylvania, not far from Philadelphia, for two weeks before the season opened. We would have time to get married.

Carol made the arrangements with a justice of the peace in Barrington and I finally went through with it. None of our parents were there. Mine were on a trip to Europe and Carol's were pretty upset with me for postponing the July wedding. They didn't want to hear my name. Carol didn't want to tell them until after we were actually married.

Carol had met my parents on a couple trips to Montreal. They all seemed to get along well, although the language barrier was a problem. My mother wasn't too pleased when I told her Carol was divorced. Being an old Catholic family, divorce wasn't looked on favorably. And since I was my parents' youngest child, maybe they worried more about me.

Even Carol's friends, Judy and Jerry Rafter, weren't at our evening wedding. Judy and Carol had been friends for a long time. Jerry had played for the Jersey Devils and was then working in the Flyers' ticket office. Carol had been after me to meet them, but I kept putting it off. Later, Carol told me if I had kept postponing our wedding, Jerry was going to punch me. But he had to catch me with my mask off.

By the time I joined the Blazers, I had gotten to know Judy and Jerry and we became good friends. Jerry is now player personnel director for the Cincinnati Stingers of the WHA—he is a good judge of hockey talent. He worked in the Blazers' front office their one season in Philly.

To show you how the Blazers were run after Jim Cooper pulled out, Jerry was told that if he associated with Carol and me he would be fired. He was part of management, I was a mere player, so we weren't supposed to even talk. We did see each other, but we had to be careful. We had planned to go on a cruise together after the season, but Bernie Brown told Jerry if he went he would be fired. So Carol and I went on the cruise by ourselves.

Several times Jerry was going to tell off Phil Watson and Brown, but I talked him out of it because I knew he liked his job.

Getting married almost cost me more than my bachelorhood. While he was working for the Philadelphia *Evening Bulletin,* John Brogan had bet me a hundred dollars that I would get married before I was twenty-five years old. John used to be at Rexy's, a restaurant in South Jersey where we went after the games, and we would start joking around. I guess John was worried when he heard I had bailed out of the big July wedding. When Carol and I were finally married, I sent John a hundred-dollar check. But he returned the check saying I should keep it as a wedding present.

The night we were married, we went over to tell Carol's parents. When they knew it was finally official, I think they were happy for us. They knew Carol was happy, and that was the most important thing for them.

I had to return to Hershey for training camp, so we didn't have a honeymoon then.

When the team returned to Philly for the season,

Carol and I and Chuckie, her son (whom I affectionately refer to as my son), who was five years old, got settled in the Barrington apartment. It was then that Carol really discovered what it is like living with a Frenchman. We still had trouble communicating.

She would ask me to get a hammer and I wouldn't know what she was talking about. Of course, when she mentioned something that involved working around the apartment and I was tired, sometimes it was convenient not to understand.

Seriously, I wanted to understand English. There were many times when we were dating that I just couldn't tell Carol in English what I was thinking. It was really torture. Your mind and heart know what you want to say, but you can't say it right in English, and it tears you up.

To help me learn English better I finally forced myself to read as much as possible. If I didn't know what a word meant, I would ask Carol, or, if we were on a road trip, I'd ask an English-speaking player.

My mother read a lot, and as I grew older I regretted not listening to her. By reading all kinds of subjects, she was able to mix easily with people from all fields.

One of my wildest experiences involved the circumstances surrounding the birth of my son, Bernie, Jr. And when I say wild, I mean "wild good," not "wild wild."

Jerry and Judy Rafter had stopped over at our apartment early one spring morning. It was actually the first time I had met Jerry. Carol said she'd make dinner, but since she was pregnant and was supposed to stay off her feet, Judy suggested that we eat at their home.

When the girls left for Judy's, Jerry and I went to play golf at Medford Lakes Country Club in New Jersey.

We were having such a great day on the links that Jerry called home to tell the girls we'd be a little late for dinner.

Now, Jerry's a great practical joker. He loves to pull gags on everyone. But I didn't know it at the time.

When he got back from the clubhouse phone, Jerry said, "Hey, Bernie, we can forget about dinner."

I said, "Why, are the girls mad because we want to stay out late?"

"Nah, they're not even home," Jerry said casually. "Judy just drove Carol to the hospital."

"Ha, ha, ha, ha. Very funny, Jerry, very funny," I said, although I wasn't too choked up with the sense of humor of a guy I had just met a few hours earlier.

"Hey, I'm not kidding," Jerry answered with a straight face. "But like I said, we don't have to worry about Judy making us dinner now. We can just keep on playing through. By the way, who's up?"

"Jerry," I shouted, "are you serious? Come on, tell me the truth. Did Judy drive Carol to the hospital?"

"I told you she did," Jerry deadpanned. "Now what do you want to do, head for West Jersey [Hospital], or keep playing?"

When I decided that Jerry wasn't joking, I let out a scream that resembled that of a love-starved moose in mating season.

Why, I yelled so loud every golfer and caddie on the course figured I had either made a hole in one or beaten Jerry in a ten-thousand-dollar Nassau.

Then seeing how overjoyed I was, I think Jerry started feeling a little guilty about his attempt at a joke.

He quickly admitted he was just pulling my leg. I'll tell you, it took a lot of willpower for me to keep from smashing my nine iron over his head.

But fortunately—for the sake of my nine iron—my willpower that afternoon was as strong as lineman John D'Amico's grip.

A couple weeks later, however, what happened was no kidding matter. It was the real thing.

I finished playing eighteen holes at Medford Lakes and drove home for dinner. As soon as I got inside, Carol said, "Hey, hon, I think this is it. I have a feeling it's going to be soon."

We kind of picked at our dinner, watched TV for a while, then went to bed. I tried to sleep, but couldn't. I guess it's tough to fall asleep when you're fully dressed. But that's the way I had sacked out. I wanted to make sure I was ready to go the second Carol gave me the word.

About one o'clock in the morning, Carol nudged me and said the labor pains were coming closer and closer together.

"Let's go," she said.

"Let's go," I sort of stammered.

My legs were shaking as I stumbled out of the apartment with Carol's suitcase in my hand.

The drive to West Jersey Hospital in Camden took about twenty minutes. I tried to make small talk, but I wasn't doing a good job at it. My heart was pounding and I was sweating so much I felt that my entire body was encased in one gigantic face mask.

When we got to the hospital, Carol's doctor, Eugene Haag of Haddonfield, New Jersey, was waiting for us. He told me not to worry and accompanied Carol to the delivery room. I paced the floor outside the maternity ward like I was tracking a caribou. Up, down, over, around. Walking, waiting, praying.

After about an hour's wait, Dr. Haag came up, slapped me on the back, and gave me the news. I was a father! What a feeling! Like winning the Vezina, Conn Smythe, and Stanley Cup all rolled into one. Nah, even greater.

I ran down the hall to see Carol. She was doing great. She was still pretty drowsy, but she had a big smile on her face. I kissed her, then flew to the nursery where Bernard Marcel Parent, Jr., was formally introduced to his old man for the first time.

I don't think he was too impressed. All he did was shriek. And he was a little young to be a Flyers' fan already, so I don't think he was screaming for my autograph.

We had called Jerry and Judy before we left for the hospital. When I got downstairs, Jerry was waiting in the lobby.

"How much does the baby weigh, Bernie?" Jerry wanted to know.

"He was fifteen pounds until they circumcised him . . . now he's down to eight," I cracked to Mr. Practical Joker.

Inside, I was proud as could be. My son. Bernie Parent, Jr. Wow, what a feeling. Even if the kid never laced on a pair of goalie pads, he was my son. And no one could ever take that away from me.

As Jerry and I stepped outside, I was still trembling like a leaf. And not a Toronto Maple Leaf.

My wife had just given birth to our son.

"Let's go celebrate, Jerry," I said to my good buddy. "The drinks and cigars are on me."

I didn't have to repeat the invitation.

Jerry and I and a lot of Jerrys we had never met

before did plenty of toasting to my new son the next few hours.

In fact, Bernie, Jr., was born on a Friday morning and we did a lot of toasting that whole weekend. Or as much of it as I can remember. You see, it's all kind of hazy to me.

I know later that Friday night, we had a bachelor party for Carol's brother, Richard Wilson, who was getting married the next day in a Pennsauken, New Jersey, church.

We drank until the early Saturday morning hours. To this day I can hardly recall anything about that wedding. And I wasn't a spectator, either. I was an usher. But if you asked me what color wedding gown Rich's bride, Arlene, had on, I'd say red. That was the predominant color I saw that afternoon and night.

We drank toasts to the bride and groom at the reception that night. And naturally, we didn't pass up the opportunity to toast the birth of Bernie, Jr., too.

Then on Sunday I visited Carol and the baby in the hospital, so Carol later informed me, and went out to do some more celebrating.

Whew, what a weekend!

I once saw Ray Milland in *The Lost Weekend* on a late night show on TV, but believe me, Ray's performance had nothing on me.

And I wasn't acting. It was the real McCoy. And I had a nearly week-long headache to prove it.

But since I also had a son named Bernard Marcel Parent, Jr., the pain in my head really didn't bother me all that much.

Our children are very important to us. I try to spend as much time with them as possible, but I'm afraid Carol winds up taking care of them most of the time. With the hockey season running from September to May, I'm away a lot. Fortunately, when the club is playing in Philly I'm around the house. When I'm not hunting, that is. I think Carol and the kids understand that I need that time alone outdoors to get my mind off hockey and relax.

When the club is on the road, I call home every night. I look forward to talking with everyone. I think the younger kids, Bernie and Kim, get a big kick out of talking with me on the phone. Chuck is now twelve and he's usually too busy to say more than "Hi." That's just the way boys that age are.

Now that the kids are older and you can do more with them, I am enjoying them more. As a result, I miss them more when I'm away. Even if we are on a hunting trip, after five, six days, I find myself missing the family. They're a big part of my life, so it's natural to miss them.

Chuck looks like he'll be a good athlete. He's playing goalie (what else?) on a team at the Centrum. I wish I could watch him play more, but if I go to the games people crowd around me and forget about the game. In Toronto it wasn't so distracting. I could just go to the rink there without many people coming around. I just hope Chuck gets a chance to show what he can do. Playing goal as Bernie Parent's son isn't the easiest thing.

It's funny, but number one on the Flyers is not number one with his sons. Rick MacLeish is Chuck's and Bernie's favorite player. They wear shirts with Ricky's number 19 on it and want his sticks. I can make ten great saves in a game, but all they want to talk about is the great goal Ricky scored.

"Did you see the great move Ricky made?" Bernie will ask me the day after a game.

"Sure I saw it," I'll tell him, pretending to be mad. "Where do you think I was, out buying popcorn?"

If we've won and Bernie's teacher says the next day, "Your father won last night," he'll say, "I don't care." It just doesn't impress him having me for a father, which is good. I want the kids to have as normal a childhood as possible.

Our home is in the Fox Hollow section of Cherry Hill. We have a nice five-bedroom Colonial on a corner with trees in the backyard. Our first home was also in Cherry Hill, in the Barclay Farms section. We moved into Barclay Farms about two months after Bernie was born. It was also a nice house, but the problem was the neighborhood was settled and we were newcomers, so we didn't make too many friends.

When we moved into Fox Hollow, everybody was new to the area. Everybody seemed more willing to meet the neighbors. We all had common problems, so everybody sort of pitched in to help each other.

The neighbors we are closest to are Mirella and Ernie Flegal, Jane and Stan Smith, Helen and Dick Wasko, and Irene and Jim McMahon.

Dr. Ernie Flegal is a heart specialist who always stops over to see me when he hears I'm sick or have been injured.

"Just want to be sure you're getting the best care," he'll say, smiling.

After our first Stanley Cup, the Smiths brought us a cake decorated like a horseshoe. Jane had taken classes to learn how to decorate cakes. I must admit I was in no condition to enjoy the cake. When Jane and Stan and their children, Bob and Gary, brought the cake to our home, I was "dozing" on the couch, after celebrating.

My meeting with Dick Wasko wasn't the smoothest. At least, he probably didn't think so. I love to joke with people. When I'm in Canada, I'll put people on by saying Americans are better than Canadians. The first time I met Dick was right after our second Stanley Cup. Right away, I went into my act, insisting that Canadians were sharper than Americans. We argued for hours and I'm afraid Dick went home thinking I was dead serious.

It's strange, but we don't socialize much with other Flyers and their wives. We all get along, but we just don't seem to get together away from the rink. The players all stop for a beer after practice, but I guess I prefer hunting with Ray to going out to dinner with other people at night.

I'm not a night owl. During the season I'm always up early because we usually practice at Penn around nine o'clock. Then if I go hunting, by about ten o'clock at night I'm tired. Carol says it's almost impossible to get me to go anywhere at night.

During the summer, I usually try to have the guys down to Wildwood so we can go fishing on my boat. But again, that's just the players and a few media buddies like Tom Brookshier, Channel 10 sports director and former pro football player. Maybe when I retire I'll feel more like going out with people.

People keep kidding me about our boat. They say I'd rather spend more time with the boat in the summer than do anything else. Well, they might be right—but just because that's really the only time I can do much fishing.

The boat is a great source of relaxation for me. I can put hockey completely out of my mind for three months. You get out in the ocean where you can't even see the shore and just concentrate on one thing: catching fish. Piloting the boat also requires concentration and skill so I can keep my mind sharp while not worrying about guys shooting pucks at me.

At the end of last summer I was thinking about buying a new boat. The thirty-three-foot Egg Harbor is fine, but a forty-six-foot Hatteras would allow me to fish farther out in the ocean and even make trips to Florida. So Howard Casper and I came up with this idea:

We went to Industrial Valley Bank in Philadelphia and asked if they'd be interested in buying the boat. I started doing commercials for IVB last year and the bank seems very happy with the results. People who open savings accounts can join a "Bernie Parent Savers Club" where they get things such as jackets and pictures.

Our plan was to charter the boat twice a week. We'd go to corporations and offer them a chance to go fishing with me. This way the boat would pay for itself quickly.

There may be nothing as boring as people talking about their pets, but I must mention our German shepherd, Tinker Bell. Since her picture was in *Time* magazine taking a nap with me, she thinks she's a celebrity.

Seriously, we all have a lot of fun with Tinker. I've always liked pets. As a child there was always a dog or cat around our house. We even had rabbits and chickens. We bought Tinker for $150 when I was with the

Blazers because I wanted security for the wife while I was on the road. Some watchdog!

The first time I came home from a trip after we got Tinker, it was about one o'clock in the morning. I knocked on the door and Carol answered it. When I looked in, Tinker stared at me for a second, then ran and hid under the bed.

Tinker is a much better watchdog now, as anyone who's wandered into our yard in Wildwood will tell you. I tried to take her hunting once when Bobby Baun went after pheasant in Canada. But Tinker distracted Bobby's Labrador retrievers too much.

Tinker is really amazing. She knows when I'll be taking a nap the day of a game. When I'm done with my steak and am finishing my coffee, she knows it's time for a nap. She goes right up to the bedroom, lies in Carol's spot, and won't move until I get up. While I'm getting dressed, we give her the steak bone to chew on.

When the weather is warm, Tinker is uncomfortable in the house, so she only lies on the bed for ten minutes or so. Then I give her a pat and say, "Go on down."

Tinker's naps have become such a part of my pre-game routine that I really miss her on the road. Maybe I should have had it written in my new contract that Tinker could travel with the club.

14

"COULD YOU PLEASE GET ME AN AUTOGRAPHED PICTURE OF JACQUES PLANTE?"

Ever since I began playing professional hockey I've been amazed at the incredibly large number of fans who take the time out to write letters and cards to me.

And just about every other player I've spoken with regarding fan mail feels the same as I do. They can't believe that so many people are interested enough to sit down and write to a total stranger.

All the guys share the same opinion about the majority of the fan mail we receive—we love it. Most fan mail is a terrific boost to our ego and also to our morale. Especially when we've had a stretch of a few bad games.

Now, when I say we love the majority of our fan mail, I mean just that. You see, besides fan mail, we all also get our share of "pan" mail.

I've been called the "greatest hockey player that ever laced on a pair of skates" in a Monday letter, and the "biggest bum on the ice" in a Tuesday postal card. No, the wife didn't send me the Monday letter.

All through my pro hockey career, I've been fortunate to be remembered in correspondence by tens of thousands of fans each season. I've never personally met 99 percent of them, yet I feel very close to them. It's a kind of strange relationship.

It would be nifty if I could say I reply to every single person who writes to me requesting an autograph or picture. But I'd be lying if I said I did. If each hockey player spent time responding to every piece of fan mail, he wouldn't log a second of ice time in any given season. He'd be too busy skating to the nearest mailbox.

Either my secretary or I do try to honor as many requests and letters as we can.

I have received fan mail of every possible shape,

220

description, variety, and size. Fan mail runs the gamut of the senders' emotions—from very serious to very funny.

Generally speaking, I'd say more youngsters than adults write. And it's not unusual to open letters signed by every student in a particular classroom. During our two drives toward the Stanley Cup in 1974 and 1975, we got a tremendous amount of support from schools in cities throughout the United States and Canada. I sometimes would wonder if these kids writing to us were doing their homework, too, but it was a pleasure hearing from them.

Because of my well-publicized admiration for hunting and fishing, I get hundreds of invitations a season through the mail to accompany a group of hunters on a trip through the woods . . . or some charter boat captain on a fishing excursion.

There are also lots of invitations from the ladies, but they're not necessarily to go hunting or fishing. The wife usually answers all of these. Ha-ha.

My mail has brought many marriage proposals, poetry and songs written about me, and the prayers of nice people of nearly every religious denomination. I love those prayers. I want to stay in as good as I can with that Man upstairs.

Lots of art-minded folks will sketch me while I'm in the net and then send me the results. You should see some of the drawings—they're very good.

Although I don't fancy myself as someone who can shell out advice to the lovelorn, evidently many romantically inclined fans envision me as a cross between "Dear Abby" and Ann Landers.

An average batch of daily mail sent to me always contains around a dozen letters from aspiring lovers who are having rough skating with the opposite sex. I hate to disappoint them, but if I offered my advice, I'd definitely wind up in Dan Cupid's penalty box for a major misconduct.

Oh, yes, another thing. Whenever I do get a chance to read my mail, there are normally a few letters filled only with gossip. Not gossip about hockey players, but gossip about the letter writers' friends, relatives, or neighbors. Now, most of the time I don't even know the person who's writing the letter, let alone their friends, relatives, or neighbors.

I mean, I try to be worldly enough to be interested in who "the widow Perkins has been seeing in Steubenville, Ohio," but I can't get all that carried away learning that "the reason old man Spatz stopped courting widow Perkins was because the Mittlelman woman makes better chocolate mousse."

Like I said, my secretary or I try to get to every piece of mail that we can. But, truthfully, that's impossible.

However, here are examples of some typical letters and cards that I never could respond to . . . and my probable replies if I had:

Dear Bernie (I shouldn't even say "Dear"),
I don't even know why I'm bothering to write to you. I'm disgusted with you.
How could you do it. You're a Canadian. You were born a Canadian. You should have the decency to play with a team in your homeland.
You could of made one of the Canadian teams keep you if you really wanted too. As good as you are, you could of called your own shot. Don't try to tell me different.

You could of stayed in Canada like you should of, but you'd rather be in Philadelfia with all those big shots.

Your no credit to the Canadian people, you traitor. Why Philadelfia?

Robert Ricard, Montreal

Dear Robert,

Why Philadelphia? Because I wanted to see if the Liberty Bell was really cracked and I love Kate Smith's voice.

Bernie,

Your team is supposed to have a reputation as the toughest in hockey.

But whenever a fight breaks out, what do you do? You just stay in the net and watch all the other guys swinging.

Don't you ever feel guilty about not fighting?

Pasquale D'Amato, Lynn, Massachusetts

Dear Pasquale,

If my name was Muhammad Ali or Joe Frazier, I'd feel real guilty. But since my name is Bernie Parent, I feel innocent.

Dear Bernie,

I think you're the greatest hockey player in the whole wide world.

We never met in person, but once at a game in the Boston Garden, you looked right at me when you were skating off the ice between the second and third period. It was two weeks ago.

I was wearing a tan turtleneck sweater and orange slacks that night. I had my hair up in a bun. I have blonde hair.

I was with my fiance that night and I think he got real jealous when you looked right at me. Do you remember me now?

Love,
Cathy Basile, Brockton, Massachusetts

Dear Cathy,
I'm not sure I remember a blonde wearing a tan turtleneck sweater and orange slacks. But I do vaguely recall some guy clenching his fists and shaking them in Turk Sanderson's direction.

Dear Bernie,
I think you are the greatest goalie that ever lived. When I grow up I want to be just like you.

Tom Stanley, Bradley, Ill.

Dear Tom,
And if I had a chance to relive my childhood, I'd want to be just like you.

Dear Sir,
I am a goalie on my street hockey team. We played six games and we won six and lost none.

I'm only 11 years old. Sometimes I'm afraid of the puck and I fall down too much.

Will you please give me some tips about stoping most of the falling and not being afraid of the puck.

I think you are one of the best goalies that ever played in the W.H.A. and the N.H.L.

Thank you,

Timmy Flynn, Philadelphia
P.S. Please Bernie, hurry!

Dear Timmy,

I'd love to help you out, but you see, when it comes to sometimes being afraid of the puck and falling down too much, we're both in the same boat.

Mr. Bernie Parent,

I love to watch you play goal for the Maple Leafs. Could you please get me an autograpphed picture of Jacques Plante? I'd appreciate it.

Martha Leeds, Toronto, Ont.

Dear Martha,

Funny you should ask. My most prized possession is an autographed picture of Jacques Plante. I really hate to part with it. But as a compromise, would you settle for an unautographed picture of Bernie Parent?

Dear Bernie Parent,

I have been watching your games when you play. I don't know which team you are on. But last year I knew what team you were on. You were on Toronto. And when ever I saw you it looked like you were wearing Jacques Plante's mask with that back thing to protect the back of your head. What is that thing that is on the back of the mask?. Your friend,

David Richards, Powell River, British Columbia
P.S. Send me your pitcure please.

Dear David,

Do you want a picture of the thing on the back of the mask or one of me?

Dear Bernie,

I play goalie for a street hockey team. And I like the style stick you use.

So could you please tell me how I could get one like yours with your number and name on it. And if you could, would you please give me an estimate on around how much it would cost.

Thank You Very Much,

George Sperber, Philadelphia

Dear George,

I really don't think I could tell you how to get a stick with my number and name on it unless you want to meet me after the game at the Spectrum and go one-on-one with me to see if you can win it from me. As far as the stick's cost estimate, why don't you contact Ed Snider. He'd probably have the answer right on the tip of his tongue.

Dear Bernie,

You are, have been, and will always be the best goalie in the W.H.A. I like you because I like your style and goaltending ability.

I want to wish you and the Blazers good luck in the playoffs.

Will you please send me a picture of you, so I can hang it on my wall with other pictures that I got out of magizines and newspapers about you?

Will you please send me a Blazer decale, if you can spare it, so I can put it on my father's car?

Your friend,

Joseph Venuto Jr., Philadelphia

Dear friend Joe,

Thanks for your good luck wishes in the play-offs. Also for your request for a Blazers' decal. I once made a request of Blazers' management when I was with them. I asked for new leg pads because the set I had been wearing wore out. When I went to try on the new pads, I discovered, much to my regret, that I had been given a set of pads for two right legs. Now, I've been accused of having two left feet on the dance floor, but never two right legs on the ice. Do you still want that Blazers' decal for your dad's car?

The letters and cards from fans come both during the season and off-season as well. As I mentioned, they're always welcomed by me and the other players.

As most everyone who knows me even casually realizes, something else that's always welcomed by me is a good steak or a good seafood dinner.

I love to eat.

Italian food, Chinese food, French food, Jewish food, Greek food, you name it, I'll eat it.

Traveling around the pro hockey circuit I've dined at some really great restaurants and had a drink or two in a few fantastic clubs.

Often, it might be disheartening to think about a long, rough road trip, but when I reflect on some of the restaurants I've had a chance to visit, I don't feel that bad.

Some of my favorites are:

The Warehouse, in Toronto. Man, I love that beef.

Joe's Steak House and Altitude 727, in Montreal. How about me? A native of Montreal who digs eating in a restaurant with the non-Canadian name of Joe's Steak House.

Hennessey's, in Chicago. You always see a gang of athletes having a few brews in there.

Lindell A.C. and Jim's Garage, in Detroit. The hamburgers are out of this world at Lindell, and the food in general is consistently super at Jim's Garage, which is near the Hotel Ponchatrain.

Stan Musial's, in St. Louis. A championship restaurant operated by a champion of a guy.

A lot of places in San Francisco. One of my favorite places is DiMaggio's on Fisherman's Wharf particularly because there's always a chance I can spot my all-time baseball hero, Joltin' Joe. Whenever we play in Oakland, the Vigilante brothers, Joe, Nick, and Jim, take me to all the fancy restaurants in Frisco. The Brothers Vigilante are mushroom growers from near San Jose and are terrific hockey fans.

Hy's, in Vancouver. The food and atmosphere are first-class.

The Buggy Whip, in Los Angeles. A real top-drawer restaurant.

The Golden Ox, in Kansas City. The steak, not the ox, is so tender and juicy in this place you could cut it with a hockey stick. I give it three stars.

The Lobster House in Cape May, New Jersey. Although it's not on the pro hockey circuit, it's a major-league restaurant. Usually when I have a good meal, I like to salute the chef with a spontaneous moose call. In the summer, I'll have dinner at the Lobster House with some of the Flyers who go out on my boat during the day. When we all let out with our moose calls, the chef probably feels complimented. But I'm not too sure about the owner, busboys, dishwashers, and waitresses. All they do is cover their ears, while the wife and the wives of the other guys we're with run for the car cringing with embarrassment.

GOALTENDING TIPS

When you use everything—glove, stick, arms, legs, skates—playing goal is a lot easier.

Catchers in baseball work hard and take a lot of physical punishment. Football linemen are often underrated and overabused. Box lacrosse goalies wear equipment that makes them look like robots, and they still get battered from head to toe.

But I am convinced that a hockey goaltender has the toughest job in sports. We wear about forty pounds of equipment that's designed to protect us, but we still must face those hard rubber disks that are fired one hundred miles per hour at us. Despite the modern equipment, my colleagues in the nets suffer broken hands, fingers, collarbones, knee damage, and bruises too numerous to count. The modern mask, pioneered by my friend and teacher, Jacques Plante, has prevented many scarred faces, but goalies can't avoid being knocked unconscious by a puck that changes direction or suddenly appears through a crowd in front of the net.

With no offense meant toward ethnic groups, hockey goalies are also a minority group in the sense that we're like the Marines: a small but proud collection linked by a common but unspoken bond. No one can know what it's like being a goalie unless he puts on the mask and pads and faces shooters whose aim is to put the puck in the net past you or through you.

I salute my brothers, young and old, who ignore danger to play the game they love.

The advantage young goaltenders have today over

when I started is better instruction. My coaches did their best to help me when I was younger, but few goalies went into coaching. As I said, unless you've been there with several opponents bearing down on you hoping to drill the puck past you, it's almost impossible to be an authority and teach a goalie.

Until recently a goalie learned by doing or exchanging tips with other goalies. It may seem odd, but on most teams the goalies will watch each other and offer advice. Here are men competing for a job, but they are willing to suggest ways the other goalie can improve. Goalies are a special breed.

What I'd like to do is pass on what I've learned to young goalies who someday hope to play major-league hockey. For those who have the talent, I hope I can make you play even better. For those who won't make the NHL, maybe you'll find some tips that make the game more enjoyable—and safer.

CHOOSING EQUIPMENT

The most important thing to remember about equipment is: Make sure it fits. I don't care if it's a twenty-dollar pair of skates or a two-hundred-dollar pair, if they don't fit you'll be miserable and probably play poorly. Remember those beautiful red goalie pads I borrowed from Gilles Boutin when I was a kid in Montreal? All I cared about was how good they looked. I completely ignored how they felt. When I put them on, I knew they were too big, but I wore them anyway and gave up something like fifteen goals. I was lucky to win the game. Maybe the other goalie was envious and kept staring at the pads instead of the puck.

Gloves. Nothing is more important than the selection of the glove. Naturally, you want the best quality glove affordable. But the question is: Does it feel comfortable? Can you catch pucks and release them quickly with the glove?

Breaking in the glove is a vital step. What I do is place five pucks in the glove pocket, wrap tape tightly around the glove, and then put it away for three or four months. Our trainers, Frank Lewis and Jimmy McKenzie, really help in ordering and keeping an eye on our gear. When I pick up the glove after it has been taped up for three or four months, it's just right and ready to use.

A glove should have a large catching pocket that lets you hold the puck securely and also makes it easy to flip it to the ice for your defensemen. Some goalies, like Plante, wear fiber-covered sponges in their gloves to protect their wrists. Plante also had a fiber cover for his thumb. Just another example of the old man thinking of everything.

Leg pads. The best length for the pads is about three inches above the knee. This varies among goaltenders, according to their size. Tall goalies, such as Ken Dryden and Gary Smith, wear pads that are halfway up their thighs. Doug Favell wears high pads, too. It all depends on your style and what makes you comfortable.

The thing to remember, though, is make sure the pads cover your knees. I learned the hard way last season when Gary Dornhoefer's shot in warm-up hit me and nearly shattered my right kneecap. It was my fault, for neglecting to wear knee pads. I also left my leg pads loose at the top to give me more flexibility.

My leg pads, like Plante's, are twenty-nine inches. NHL rules limit the length of pads to thirty-six inches. Also, the pads can't be more than ten inches wide.

Knee pads. After what happened to me in last year's play-offs, I strongly endorse knee pads. Another thing I learned from the old man is anytime you get hurt you should fix your equipment so it won't happen again. If you go back on the ice wearing equipment the same as when you got hurt, you've got to be stupid. The knee pads we wear are similar to those worn by basketball players with tender knees. They cost about six dollars a pair. I don't wear them when I'm breaking in new leg pads because the leg pads are so stiff they make it tough to move. Put on knee pads in such a situation and you'd feel like you were on stilts. Most players feel awkward when they first wear knee pads, but they soon get used to them. One suggestion is: Use an elastic band below the knee to hold the pads up. Tape is bad because it won't stretch. Wearing tape will make your legs feel as if they're in a vise.

Arm pads. After many games writers like Walt Burrows of the *Courier Post* in South Jersey will ask which shots caused the bruises on my arms.

"Shots didn't do that," I'll say, pointing to the purple-and-yellow bruises. "That's where my wife bit me last night."

The truth is goalies do receive a lot of bruises from pucks. Our bodies would look much worse if it weren't for the shoulder-pad adjustment Plante showed me. Regular shoulder pads protect only the outside of the upper arm. Plante sewed a piece of felt covered with some fiber inside the arm sleeve. To protect our elbows, he and I use a sponge.

The old man also changed the old-style shoulder pads, which were in one piece. He'd tie the arm pads to the chest protector with laces to allow more movement.

Chest protector. A well-fitting protector extends to the waist and doesn't bind the shoulders. The old man told me to pick a protector that had flaps that covered my shoulders.

Years ago, the NHL passed a rule requiring goalies to wear the protector inside their pants. This was in the days when no equipment could show outside the uniform. Today's protectors are thin enough to be tucked inside the pants, although Plante still advises goalies to wear the protector outside the pants. This way the goalies will find it easier to move.

How to wear the protector is one of the few areas where I disagree with the old man. I wear my protector inside the pants because it makes me look thinner. All the other gear makes goalies look fat enough. I shudder to think how monstrous a big football player like Mean Joe Greene of the Pittsburgh Steelers would look in goalie's gear. Seriously, I just find having the protector inside the pants more comfortable.

Skates. Buying a good pair of skates is probably tougher than buying shoes. You'll wear skates for sixty minutes, plus warm-up. Once the game begins, you want to forget you're even on skates. The game is tough enough so you don't want to be bothered by ill-fitting skates. Imagine the agony someone like Willie (Puddinhead) Jones went through. I'm told that Jones, the third-baseman of the Philadelphia Phillies' last pennant winner in 1950, had such bad feet that he'd say, "My feet only hurt when they touch the ground."

Hockey players frequently suffer sore feet, but it's

usually only when they're breaking in new skates. Skate companies, like Bauer, the skate I use, take such good care of us now that we don't worry about picking skates that are the wrong size.

The best thing to do when trying on skates is push your heel back in the boot to guarantee a snug fit. Youngsters should buy skates the same size as their shoes. As they grow older, they should buy skates that are a size smaller than their shoes.

A good salesman will show you how to lace skates properly. It's difficult to generalize about lacing skates, since people have individual preferences. The only advice an outsider can give is: Skates shouldn't be laced too tight or too loose. You'll quickly know if the laces are too tight. Since goalies crouch much of the game, there is pressure on the top of their feet. Tightly laced skates will make you react like Puddinhead Jones. You'll be saying, "My feet only hurt when I'm wearing these damn skates!"

Another important thing about skates is keeping the blade in playing shape. On many boys' teams you'll probably have to do it yourself or have people at the rink do it. NHL players are fortunate that most of our trainers are skilled at preparing skates the way we like. Our trainers even carry a skate-sharpening machine to road games. But even in the NHL many goalies like to take care of dulling the blade's edge. You learn how many times to pass the stone over the edge to get the perfect dullness. I usually pass the stone over the blade's edge six times.

One more suggestion: Always wipe off the skate blade after using them to prevent rusting. And never leave skates near a heater. The heat will shrink the boot.

No one expects a goalie to skate as smoothly as Guy Lafleur or as fast an Yvan Cournoyer. (I've often wondered how fast such super skaters would go if they had to wear our gear.) But goalies should work on skating well for fifteen or twenty feet, the distance required to control loose pucks.

When your team is practicing those dreaded "stops and starts"—from goal line to blue line and back, then to the red line and back—bear down and work hard. Goalies must be able to take short, quick strides, stop on the outside skate, then skate backward. Learn how to be agile around the net. You'll help yourself and your team.

Sticks. Obviously a stick's size and weight depend on your build. Someone like Ken Dryden, who is 6′4″, needs a bigger stick than Rogie Vachon, who is 5′7″.

The stick's weight also depends on what you feel comfortable handling. I like my stick not too heavy and not too light. Sounds like I'm ordering a steak, eh? Not too rare and not too well done. If a stick is too light, it will feel like a feather and you might not keep it on the ice. The Sherwood Company takes good care of my sticks. They always feel just right.

Goalies should also be concerned about the lie of their sticks. Most stand-up goalies use a fourteen or fifteen lie. My sticks have a thirteen lie. A higher lie forces you to stand more erect.

All the well-fitting, good-looking equipment money can buy won't help a goalie if he lacks one essential ingredient: *courage*. If, even with full equipment on and a good team in front of him, a goalie is continually afraid of injury, he should ask himself how much he really wants to play.

We're all nervous at times. Some of us admit it or show it. Others conceal it. But it's similar to what they say about a soldier: If he isn't afraid before a battle, he'd better check to see if he hasn't already joined the big honor guard in the sky.

As I've said, there are days I worry about injuries, so in practice I ask the guys to fire shots at me until the fear has passed. I've never heard a goalie who has been in the game awhile admit he was scared. He might be afraid of losing or having a bad game, but not of getting hurt. After you've played in the nets awhile you know the dangers. Guys who are afraid get out of the game long before they can turn pro. And I don't think kids think about injuries. They're having too much fun.

If a goalie was worried about the puck hurting him, Plante would tell him to hunch up his shoulders, move slowly toward the shooter, and lean forward. Doing this helps keep your stick on the ice and usually makes the goalie overcome his fear.

PLAYING THE GAME

Most youngsters who have baseball experience are surprised when we tell them at hockey schools to "let the puck play you." In baseball, fielders are drilled in not letting the ball play them. They are told to charge a ground ball to prevent the ball from taking short or bad hops away from them.

Perhaps the best advice I can give young goaltenders is to learn to use every part of your body to stop shots.

Many times you'll hear fans say, "Geez, what a great glove that goalie has. He's really quick." What people overlook is how the goalie is making other saves. Say, a goalie faces twenty-nine shots in a game. Maybe he catches ten. That means he made nineteen other saves without using his glove. That's the kind of goalie who impresses me. It shows he learned how to use his arms, legs, and skates to block shots. When you use everything you can, playing goal is a lot easier.

A good example of a goalie not relying on his glove or stick occurred in our Stanley Cup semifinal series with the New York Islanders in the 1974–75 season. It was the third game, and my first one back from my knee injury. We had won the first two games at the Spectrum, with Wayne Stephenson in the nets. I knew people would be watching me closely to see if I had fully recovered from the knee problem.

Late in the first period, André St. Laurent, the Islanders' hustling little center, fired a twenty-footer that had me beat until I threw out my left leg and deflected it at the last second. It was the kind of quick shot that I couldn't get my stick or glove on.

There were two other shots in that game that are good examples to learn from.

Part of letting the puck play you if forcing the shooter to make the first move. If the goalie commits himself first, he's usually at the mercy of the shooter.

In the second period, Billy Harris came in on me. Harris is a big guy (6'2", 195) who moves well and knows what to do with the puck. I thought he would shoot at the far side, so I made my move. He held the puck a split second, then shot on the short side. Lucky for me, his shot hit the post and bounced away.

We won the game 1–0 on a goal by Reggie Leach. Reggie was carrying the puck up the right side, with Dave Lewis, the Islanders' defenseman, standing up with him. Reggie said he saw Lewis was to his right, so he suddenly cut to the left toward center ice, skated in on Glenn Resch, and scored on a high backhander. When Reggie got around Lewis, Resch skated pretty far out of the net.

Later, Resch admitted he came out too far, but he felt he had to cut down Reggie's shooting angle.

Resch was right about reducing Reggie's room to shoot, but I've learned that it's not good to roam out too far from the crease. Once your motion is forward there is no way you can move your feet or arms sideways. The only way to make the save is with your body—and the shooter has to cooperate by putting the puck where your body is. I tell our shooters that when they see the goalie come out they should keep the puck on the ice.

Plante always said to stay on the edge of your crease. This way you've got balance, you're in control, and can move in any direction with confidence.

During games I try to watch the other team's goaltender. It doesn't matter whom we're playing or what the goalie's record is. Every goalie has his strong point.

Take Bobby Taylor, which I wish some NHL team would do. The Chief hasn't played much in two seasons, but I'k sure he could help some NHL team. Since the Chief hasn't had the chance lately to show what he can do, people probably forget that he is very good at poke-checking the puck away from shooters. I've tried for years and years to improve my poke-checking, which comes in handy when you're trying to beat a shooter to a loose puck in front of the net, but I haven't made much progress. I can do it, but not as well as the Chief.

Maybe the Chief spent some time with Plante learning how to poke-check. The old man's advice was good:

First, make sure the shooter is even with the net before you throw your stick out toward him. Try to play the puck with the bottom of the stick blade. If you should hook the puck, it might slide under you as you pull the stick back.

Don't worry about tripping the puck carrier with your stick. It's you against him.

Try to remember to keep one leg behind you to guard against the shooter scoring on the short side. And hold the stick handle at the very end.

There are times when I don't watch the other team's goalie. This happens after I've made what I consider a bad play, but the opponent didn't score. As the action moves to the far end of the ice, I'll try to recall the play where they almost scored. I'll ask myself, "What did I do wrong?" To the fans its looks like I'm just clearing the ice chips from the crease, but I'm thinking, too. Maybe I moved too quick, or took my eye off the puck. Then I'll try to file away in my mind not to make the same mistake again.

I've heard that Tony Esposito and Gary Smith work on their concentration by breaking up the periods into five-minute segments. This way the pressure doesn't seem as constant. My way is to hold my own clinic and go over what I'm doing.

Defending against two-on-ones. We're playing the Rangers and Jean Ratelle and Rod Gilbert break over the red line with only Joe Watson back for us. How can we stop them?

The first thing every goalie learns in this situation is: The goalie takes the puck and puck carrier while the defenseman takes the other man who might receive a pass.

Both the goalie and the defenseman hope the puck is passed. The odds are on your side then because, in this case, Ratelle might make a bad pass. Or the puck might hit something. If Ratelle fakes a pass to Gilbert and I go with the fake, I'm in big trouble. My biggest wish then is that Ratelle slips and falls.

The defenseman should stay between the two forwards and, if possible, pressure the puck-carrier into making a pass. If you're close to the ice, you might hear the goaltender yell, "Stand up!" or "Stay up!" to his defenseman. In other words, I'd want Joe Watson to stay between the two scoring threats and try not to screen the goalie's view.

Breakaways. Follow the goalie's primary rule of not committing yourself first. Move out to cut down the angle, but don't stray too far from the crease or you'll be helpless as the shooter skates past you for an easy goal.

Another tip in this predicament is to keep your eyes on the puck. In some cases, like when you're on the ice and can't see the puck, you follow the shooter's eyes. But when you have a clear view of the shooter, don't take your eyes off the puck.

I have a few tricks I use when I'm faced with a breakaway or two-on-one, but I won't reveal them until I retire. Guys such as Jacques Lemaire, Garry Unger, and Gil Perreault are enough trouble without me giving them some of my secrets.

Handling the puck. When I was growing up, coaches would tell goalies not to catch any shots that would miss the net. The coaches were afraid the goalie might mishandle the puck and it would drop in the net. This thinking makes sense, but Plante suggested I catch anything I could safely reach. His thinking was: Why let the puck hit the glass or boards? You never know where it might go. When you catch the puck, especially when your team is shorthanded, you're in control.

Try to remember to bring your stick and backhand glove (or blocker) behind your catching glove when the puck is at your chest. This way you'll have a little insurance should you mishandle the puck.

Stopping the puck behind the net isn't as easy as it looks. I'm sure when Eddie Giacomin or Gilles Gilbert stops the puck behind the net, some fans think, "Isn't that nice—he's taking a little skate to ease the pressure." Bah! It takes agility and judgment to know when to leave the crease and where to leave the puck.

Youngsters shouldn't move from in front of the net unless the puck is shot in from beyond the blue line. As a young goalie develops more skill and confidence, he can skate behind the net under other conditions. The best place to leave the puck is about six inches from the boards. This way a teammate swinging in behind the net has room to handle the puck easily without going near the goal cage.

Communication. Talking to teammates on the ice is very important. The Flyers talk all the time. If a defenseman is swinging in behind the net, I might tell him to keep the puck. If someone is chasing him, I'll tell him to pass it around the boards. The defensemen and forwards are always yelling to each other. Ricky Mac-Leish has often said that the success of his line is due to Gary Dornhoefer and Ross Lonsberry talking to him on the ice.

For some reason, there are teams who hardly ever say a word on the ice. I've wondered if they think someone will say "Shhh!" because they are too loud.

Very often fans will see the goalie and his teammates confer before a face-off. Knowing where each man will be on the face-off is important. There's nothing like a goal direct from a face-off to crush a team's spirit.

Plante used to remind his centermen to be careful if the other center was facing off with his forehand facing Plante. You don't want the other center drawing the puck to his forehand for a quick shot.

I also remind our players to be certain they look at me before the linesman drops the puck. I'm standing in the net and can see everything. If we aren't ready, I'd be the first one to notice.

Criticizing teammates. Very rarely do you hear of a goaltender, even on a losing team, publicly berating his teammates for playing poorly. I'm sure there have been times Gilles Meloche has been tempted to pop off about the way the California Seals were playing. Ron Low and Michel Belhumeur had to be mad at the way the Washington Capitals were going in the 1974–75 season. But if any of them ever hit the ceiling, it's a good bet it was done in the dressing room with only the team around.

What usually happens is the team has a meeting.

The team leaders get up and say, "Look, we've got to change things around." Then they'll ask if anything is bugging the players. When the air is cleared, even poor teams often play well, at least for a couple games.

When I was with Boston there were times I felt like sounding off. But I was only a twenty-year-old kid playing with men thirty and thirty-five years old. What could I say?

The only time good players get upset is when teammates are doing things off the ice that affect the way they produce in games. That's the time to call a meeting and straighten things out.

Several fans have asked me if players ever let down in front of certain goalies by, say, not blocking shots they could reach. Maybe the goalie is living the kind of life that hurts him and the team on the ice. Or maybe the goalie is just hard to get along with. Plante was never voted "most popular player" by his teammates, but the players never stopped producing in front of him. I've never seen or heard of a team slacking off and making it tough for a goalie. Once the game starts you're in front of eighteen thousand people, you're a man, so you want to produce regardless of what you feel about your teammates.

Luck. Flyers' fans like Joe Bigenis, a Philadelphia policeman who fishes out of Wildwood, have asked how big a part luck plays in a goalie's game. Sure we have to be lucky sometimes. If a Bobby Orr or Jean Pronovost of Pittsburgh makes a good move on me but doesn't score, luck has to be involved.

But I've always felt that mistakes result more from underestimating yourself than from someone getting lucky. If a goalie plays his system, he's got 75 percent on his side and the shooter has 25 percent. Put yourself in the shooter's skates: He has only one or two seconds to make up his mind because one of our guys will be closing in on him. Ah, but, the goalie makes an error, then the odds go down to 50-50.

Sometimes, no matter how well you play your system, the other team will score. In the 5–1 game we lost to the Islanders in the '75 semifinals, Jude Drouin came down the left side and got around our defenseman. I moved out a little to cut down the angle, had my stick on the ice and my glove ready. But Drouin still scored, hitting the far upper corner of the net. Give the guy credit: It was a good shot. There was nothing else I could do. However, nine times out of ten that shot won't go in if I'm following my system.

Gerry Hart had a winning goal in that series that many people wondered about. Hart's goal gave the Islanders a 2–1 win to even the series at three games apiece. We had to go back to the Spectrum, rush in Kate Smith, and get three quick goals to win the game 4–1 and the series.

Hart is a gutsy little defenseman who doesn't score many goals. But he got his own rebound past me early in the third period of the sixth game for a 2–1 lead that stood up. Later, writers and the platoon of radio people with tape recorders asked if it bothered me to have a low-scoring defenseman like Hart score the winning goal.

I told them it doesn't matter who scores—all the goals irritate me. Hart's goal just proved that you have to respect whomever you're playing against. That's why the challenge is so great in the NHL.

Hart's goal is something for goalies everywhere to

remember. No matter whom you're playing, don't be overconfident. You need confidence, but don't underestimate anybody on the other team. Be ready at all times because anybody on the ice can score if you get careless.

Freddie Shero and I like to talk a lot at banquets so we don't eat too much.

Notice my powerful swing and riveted eyes. I had all it takes to become a mediocre baseball player.

Left above: The 1973 Flyers got all spiffed up for a dinner honoring Bobby Clarke as the Hart Trophy winner. We hardly resemble the Broad Street Bullies, more like a Parcheesi team.

Left below: The '74 Flyers tried other sports, too — like a benefit softball game at Veterans Stadium.

The Flyer wives held a dinner to raise money for the battle against breast cancer. Front row: Wahnita Lonsberry, Isabelle Leach, Cathy Clement, Genette Dupont, Maryann Saleski, Sheila Crisp. Second row: Lynn Kindrachuk, Heather Kelly, Carolyn MacLeish, Nedina Stephenson, Cheryl Dornhoefer, Carol. Top row: Diane Bladon, Cathy Schultz, Mary Ann Watson, Sandy Clarke, Jenny Barber .

One of Fred Shero's pre-game meetings;
except that usually we listen .

During the "fog" game I was able to take a rare rest. It should happen more often — the rest I mean.

We won this game so it was pretty easy to answer questions.

Before a game, the camera captures a good shot.

Here is the captain and his yacht. I love fishing and the fun we all have on the boat.

The Parents pose in their living room. Around me are Chuck, Carol, Kim, and Bernie, Jr.

"HOCKEY
IS A
VIOLENT
GAME"

The season leading to our second Stanley Cup was full of pressure, but it had been exciting. Many good things happened to us as a team and as individuals.

In my case, *Time* magazine assigned a reporter, Bob Lewis, to follow the team for a while. The magazine used my picture on their cover, marking the first time to my knowledge that a hockey player had made *Time*'s cover. Of course, I was wearing my goalie mask. All you could see was my eyes.

When the magazine came out, people like Don Wilno, the Trenton (New Jersey) *Times* hockey writer, kidded me, saying for all he knew that could be Tinker behind the mask.

I thought the *Time* story was well done and was good for hockey. They used several color action photos plus some of the family and me taking a nap with Tinker. You can imagine the kidding I took about that picture.

The *Time* story also discussed violence in hockey. There were pictures of guys fighting and bleeding. Cripes, you hear "violence in hockey" almost as much as "crime in the streets." Crime is a helluva lot more serious than violence in hockey. No one is forcing people to fill the NHL arenas, so we must be doing something they want to see.

People like action and contact. Hockey is a fast physical game, so people come to see it. I don't believe most hockey fans want to see fights. The real fans appreciate the skating, shooting, checking, and, I hope, the goaltending.

I'll admit there is some violence in hockey. There are some mean S.O.B.'s who will do anything on the ice. I can't stand guys who use their sticks. A guy like Ted

Green used to do the same things in practice he did in the game when he was with Boston.

Fans in other arenas hate Dave Schultz because he stirs things up, but they remember that he never uses his stick. He always drops his gloves.

The only time Schultzie used his stick was once against Boston when Terry O'Reilly blind-sided him, knocking him goofy for a few seconds. When Dave got up, he felt humiliated. He skated over to the penalty box where O'Reilly was sitting and swung his stick, But hit the boards. Even our guys didn't like seeing that. If Dave had hit O'Reilly, Terry Crisp said he wouldn't want to be associated with Dave. But I don't think Dave was himself when he swung the stick.

The Dave Forbes case attracted a lot of attention. I never saw the tapes of what Forbes did to Henry Boucha, who was then with the Minnesota North Stars. But from what I heard, it was pretty bad. As they sat in the penalty box Forbes threatened to shove his stick down Boucha's throat. As soon as they both left the box, Forbes swung and the butt of his stick caught Boucha in the eye. I think what upset people and caused charges to be pressed against Forbes is that when Boucha went down he was bleeding heavily but Forbes kept hitting him.

Perhaps like Schultzie, Forbes had lost control of himself for a few minutes. I'm sure Forbes went through hell during the trial in Minneapolis, but maybe the whole thing was good for hockey. Maybe now guys will think twice before unnecessarily roughing somebody up.

The NHL Players Association has recommended a

crackdown on players for intent-to-injure acts. If the league does punish players severely for injuring others or attempting to injure, guys will know they'll have to watch what they do. The game needs contact, but not senseless mayhem.

For the first time in the *Time* story I talked about some fears I have. For instance, I hate practices. I'm actually scared going out on the ice. It's just not fun.

Most men get up in the morning, have breakfast, kiss their families goodbye, and drive to either an office or factory where they have relatively safe jobs.

Hockey goalies have a cup of coffee, kiss the family goodbye, then drive to a chilly arena where an hour or so later players are shooting pucks at them at ninety to a hundred miles an hour. Sure we get used to it, but when we think about what we're doing it's no wonder we have to keep checking to see if we're carrying a full deck.

It is almost impossible to explain what it's like to face a puck that's soaring at you as fast as a Nolan Ryan pitch. I think race-car drivers have the same problem trying to tell people what it's like traveling at 180 miles an hour. You have to be there to understand.

When I'm worried about facing shots, I ask the guys to just fire pucks at me until what I'm doing doesn't bother me. That's why I practice hard because what you do in practice is what you'll do in a game.

It's odd, but once a game starts I forget about the shots and getting hurt. In a game it becomes a challenge: me against the shooter, us against them. When I make a save, it's rewarding because I have beaten the shooter. I have won—at least for the moment.

But sometimes a goaltender's biggest helpers are

the goalposts. If you're in another building, like Buffalo, and a couple of their shots hit the posts and don't go in, the crowd thinks you're lucky. Sure it's luck, but I don't know a goaltender who would ask for a rule change making shots that hit the posts count as goals. If those posts were human, we'd treat them to steak dinners.

In the game we beat Buffalo 4-1. During the 1975 finish a shot by Rick Martin from point-blank range got past me. Later I told the writers that I had asked the post to take the shot, but it didn't. I guess I shouldn't tell stories like that. People think goaltenders are crazy enough without me admitting I talk to the pipes.

I'm not the only goaltender who shows affection for his "helpers." When one of our shots in the 1975 semifinals hit the post, Chico Resch, the Islanders' goalie, turned around and kissed the post. I know just how he felt.

Another good thing that happened to me in the 1974-75 season was an award from Seagram's as Hockey's most proficient player. Seagram's had commissioned a computer organization to determine who was the most effective performer in each major pro sport. The award was worth $10,000, which was an unexpected bonus.

Some developments on the road to Stanley Cup II weren't so good, like injuries. I have been fortunate over the years in avoiding serious injuries. But in the 1974-75 season I had a bruised chest, a pulled thigh muscle, a pinched nerve in the neck, and a knee bruise that could have been very serious. Cripes, I must be getting old.

The potentially serious injury occurred in a warm-up prior to our Stanley Cup semifinal series with the New

York Islanders. I had suffered a pinched neck nerve during practice after we had finished beating Toronto in four straight. I wasn't sure whether I would play against the Islanders. I thought I'd take the warm-up and see how I felt.

While I was stopping shots, Gary Dornhoefer wound up and let one go that hit just below my right kneecap. I hope I never know how it feels to be shot, but this had to be close to it. I tumbled to the ice and thought, "Cripes, something is broken." It hurt like hell.

Dorny and Jimmy McKenzie, our assistant trainer, helped me to the dressing room where I changed and was taken to Pennsylvania Hospital for X rays. Joe Kadlec, the Flyers' press relations director, told Carol about the injury. She was in the wives' lounge.

Dr. Edward Viner, our new team physician, who with Dr. John Wolf, our orthopedic surgeon, gives us a great medical team, told me that it was just a bad bruise to the tendons and bone. What a relief! As I said later, I got hit in the right place. Another inch or so and the kneecap could have been shattered. Just to clear Dorny, it was my fault because I have always worn my knee pads loose at the top. The pad was flopping loose and not giving me protection when Dorny's shot hit me.

17

A
LIFETIME
DEAL

It's a nice feeling waking up every morning knowing you're set for life

That near-tragic injury before the Islanders' play-off game ties in with the lifetime contract arrangement I signed with the Flyers last summer.

As far as I know, when it was announced it was a totally new idea in player contracts. The reason I wanted such a deal is my increasing worry over injury. As I have grown older, my philosophy of the game has changed. Before, my fear wasn't of getting hit, but of losing. I thought more about having a bad game than of injury.

Now that I'm more mature, my thinking has expanded and I'm more concerned about taking care of my family and myself. I appreciate life more than I used to. I want my family to have nice things and I'd like to do the things I like when I'm finished playing.

I'm really not all that superstitious, even though a lot of athletes are.

Oh, I guess I have my share of things I do for good or bad luck. But I'm not a fanatic about too many of them, particularly on the ice.

But there's one thing I do—almost religiously.

Nearly every good-luck token or souvenir I get during the regular season I stuff inside my shaving kit.

You know, people will walk up to me and hand me all kinds of things when I'm coming off the ice or leaving the Spectrum.

And instead of throwing them away, or taking them home and storing them in a box in the basement or something like that, I automatically put them in my shaving kit. I guess I do it subconsciously, but I do it always.

Carol keeps on pleading with me to take all the trinkets out of the kit, but for some reason, I just won't.

Then, at the end of each hockey season, when I'm out fishing Carol goes through my kit and discards all my little good-luck charms. Well, she doesn't really discard them, she actually puts them in a big box. She doesn't dare try to jinx me.

Last summer, besides my shaving cream, razor, and blades, Carol also discovered about a hundred items . . . including a brown rock, a medal of the Statue of the Infant of Prague, and around twenty-five assorted gum wrappers.

Late last season, Howard and I were talking over dinner one night at his country club—Radnor Valley. The club is a beautiful place situated in Philadelphia, in the traditional Main Line area, not far from Villanova University. Going to Radnor Valley is always a pleasure for me because the people are so nice. There's no fuss or anything. They just treat me like Howard's friend.

While we ate dinner I mentioned to Howard that I would like more security than a five-year contract. What would happen to me if I suffered a serious injury like the one that almost knocked me out of the play-offs? I would be paid on the remainder of my contract, and then, after all the years and sweat and worry I had put into hockey, I'd be on my own with no security. The game has been good to me, but I think I've put something worthwhile into it, too. I wanted to have something when I was done.

My philosophy of life has been "you're dead a long time" so work hard, then enjoy yourself. Dedicate yourself to accomplishing something, which I've done and the Flyers have done. We won't stop, but when we are through with hockey we're entitled to enjoy some benefits.

After I explained to Howard what I was after he said he would come up with a plan and then present it to Mr. Snider. The plan is basically this:

If I stop playing after the next seven seasons, I get more than I ever made in Toronto tax free each year for the rest of my life. For each year I play after the seven years, the annual total goes up. The contract is guaranteed by the Flyers, the league, and Lloyd's of London. Should I die prematurely, the family will be provided for financially for twenty years.

Hey, with that kind of money a man can buy a lot of gas for the boat and a few warehouses filled with Lite beer.

When Howard proposed the idea of the lifetime contract, he said Mr. Snider "wasn't too pleased." Salaries and expenses for hockey clubs, especially a winner like the Flyers, have skyrocketed since the WHA started (thanks in part to me). I'm sure the last thing the owners want to hear is another request for more money.

Howard said Mr. Snider changed his opinion a little after Howard explained that such a lifetime arrangement would guarantee the Flyers a contented player who is one of the best at his job. Mr. Snider and Gil Stein, the club's attorney, studied the proposal, revised it, and finally agreed to it.

As I've said, Mr. Snider is very aware of how the players feel about security. He said that while our plan was unique, and expensive, he was considering the same plan for Bobby Clarke and other players.

Reaction to the lifetime deal was generally favorable, although some people questioned how it would affect my play. Players in professional sports have been known to coast a little after receiving multi-year or no-cut contracts. As I've said, there are some "floaters" in the NHL.

I tried to make it clear that the new contract would not discourage me from trying my best. It's a nice feeling waking up every morning knowing you are set for life. No more worries about investments. If they come through, fine. If they don't, I don't have to worry. But I'm from the old school in that I believe whatever I do in life I should try my best. If I take people out deep-sea fishing and we haven't caught anything, I'll stay out until three o'clock in the morning trying to get them some fish. I feel like I owe them something after they've spent money to go out.

With hockey, when I put on the pads I don't think about the contract. When Bobby Orr or Marcel Dionne or Guy Lafleur are winding up to shoot a puck, you'd better not be thinking about money or else they'll hit you right in the dollar sign. I still want to produce.

The philosophy of wanting to do your best runs in our family. My mother and father told us to always try hard. You may not succeed every time, but if you are honest with yourself, people will be fair with you in the long run. If you are honest, your talent will take over and carry you as far as it can.

Looking at my job, I figure I work hard nine months a year and have three months off. In those three months I want to enjoy myself.

Many times during the summers I have sat on the back porch of our house in Wildwood, looked at my boat docked just a few feet away on the bay, and thought about how fortunate I am. When I look around and see everything I have, it makes me want to produce on the ice, during the nine months I'm working. I don't think that feeling will change until it's time to take off the mask and pads for the last time.

In the 1975–76 season we are faced with our biggest challenge. We can become the first team since Toronto in the early sixties to win three straight Stanley Cups. Very few teams in any sport lately have won three consecutive championships. Oakland, with three World Series victories, is the only one I can think of. The Miami Dolphins got close, winning two straight Super Bowls.

All our players are still hungry. We still want to win. After struggling to get to the top, your pride makes you want to stay there.

To prepare for this critical season, I relaxed in the way I enjoy most: hunting and fishing.

In late August, some friends, including Bob Martineau and Mike Lemieux, left for Labrador to hunt caribou. The caribou is a wild reindeer that roams in herds from Newfoundland as far as Alaska. Where we were going in Labrador was parallel to the southern tip of Alaska and was eighteen hundred miles from Philadelphia. It was supposed to be too cold even for the caribou, but while we were there it was around 75° during the day. That's 75° above zero. Old-timers in the area told us they had never experienced weather like that before in late August, early September. People at the Schefferville airport said that in the winter there it is 35° to 45° below zero. Sometimes the wind chill makes it 125° below!

One part of hunting I like is preparing for the trip.

Before I left Wildwood, I gathered all my gear. We even set up the tent in the backyard, near the docks. The day before I left, Claude and Grandpop Campbell helped me take the tent down and pack it. Grandpop Campbell is Carol's grandfather. He and Grandmom Campbell live in Clementon, New Jersey, but they spend a lot of time with us in Cherry Hill. They're fun to be around. Grandpop is quite a hockey fan. He always has advice for Freddie Shero and Keith Allen.

When we were ready for the trip, Claude and I drove to Montreal. Then our hunting party drove for fifteen hours to Seven Islands, Quebec, at the mouth of the St. Lawrence River. Then we took a fifteen-hour train ride north to Schefferville, Quebec. From there it was a two-hour flight to the lake where the two planes carrying us landed.

When those who know how I dislike flying ask how I could stand a single-engine plane that landed on a lake, I'd tell them:

"I prayed a lot."

The only thing that really worried me was on these trips the plane drops you off, then returns fourteen days later. You have no communication with the outside world, so if something delayed the plane in returning, we wouldn't know. One hunting party had to stay six days longer than scheduled because weather prevented the plane from landing. As it turned out, our pickup was no problem.

I bagged my caribou on our fourth day isolated by the lake. We were walking through the woods around noon when I spotted the caribou. I tapped Bob on the arm and pointed to the caribou about seventy-five yards away. The animal was standing still in a small clearing with the sun peering through the trees. Our

269

prey was easy to line up. One shot did it, then we had to carry the caribou back to our lodge. You have to cut the animal into quarters, tie it to your backpack, and walk to where you're staying.

The caribou I got weighed four hundred pounds and its antlers had a spread of fifty-seven inches. I'm having its head mounted to go in our den at home where I also have a deer's head mounted.

Our den is also decorated with many of my trophies and hockey pictures. People have suggested to Carol that it's odd for a goaltender to have all these hockey reminders so visible. They think I'd prefer "getting away from it all." Carol just replies that I probably only notice the deer head and marlin that I also have mounted.

I'm sure people who find hunting cruel will think that other outdoorsmen and I are beasts. Well, my main thought on hunting is that they butcher cattle every day, but few people complain. Nobody protests when fish are caught.

Shooting the animal is not the big thrill for me. What I enjoy is getting ready for the trip, arriving where we're going to hunt, and having peace of mind. There's nothing like waking up with the sunrise and hearing the sounds of the forest. Spending your days hunting and fishing away from traffic jams and phone calls and slapshots is heaven on earth to me.

The rest of the trip we hunted small game and fished for trout. The plane picking us up arrived on time, and a couple days later I was back on the University of Pennsylvania rink's ice, stopping pucks. End of vacation, time to return to the pressurized life of a hockey goaltender, a life of challenges, excitement, and danger.

The danger of injury surfaced again near the end of

training camp. Like the knee injury I suffered before the Islanders' Stanley Cup semifinals, this latest problem was one that could have ended my hockey career. This time, in fact, I was more worried than ever about an injury.

One morning shortly after a workout began at the University of Pennsylvania, I turned my head as I blocked a shot and suddenly felt a sharp pain in the neck. I tried to continue, but it hurt like hell so I had to leave the ice. Frank Lewis, our trainer, checked me over and said I should see Dr. John Wolf, the club's orthopedic surgeon.

Dr. Wolf is associated with Abington Memorial Hospital in Abington, Pennsylvania, a pleasant suburb just north of Philadelphia. He examined me at the hospital and suggested I wear a neck brace for a couple days. He thought a pinched neck nerve was causing the pain.

After two days at home wearing the neck brace —and pajamas—the pain hadn't subsided so Dr. Wolf put me in traction in Abington.

The next few days were physically the most miserable of my life. I had felt great during training camp and couldn't wait to start the new season. Now I was propped up in a hospital bed with weights and pulleys attached to my head. As long as I was in traction I felt okay, but as soon as I moved my head the sharp pain made me want to scream.

After a week in the hospital, we finally decided a myelogram should be taken. This is not the most comfortable procedure: dye injected in the spinal canal reveals on X-rays where disc damage might be. Fortunately, in my case the myelogram showed a bone spur pressing on the sixth nerve and a piece of disc putting pressure on the seventh nerve. It was fortunate because even though it meant the first major surgery of my life, the less complicated of two operations could be done. The doctors said if they had had to operate from the front to fuse the discs, my vertical head movement would have been limited. Conclusion: no more hockey.

Dr. Wolf and two neurosurgeons performed the two-and-one-half-hour surgery on a Tuesday in mid-October. Everything seemed to go well and they predicted I'd be back with the team in another month.

I hope they're right. I know Wayne Stephenson can do a good job while I'm recuperating, but I want to be back with the team. We've won two Stanley Cups together and proven we're the best. We want to do it again.

Some people might think this latest setback would discourage me. I admit it was a scary experience, but to me it's just another challenge. And as I've said, I like challenges.

Will the Flyers win their third straight Stanley Cup?

Ha, if I knew the answer, there would be no reason to play over a hundred games. No one can guarantee a championship. There are many good teams in the NHL and all have a shot at the cup.

But we have tasted champagne from the Stanley Cup twice. We know the exhilarating feeling only a player on a Stanley Cup-winner can appreciate.

The good teams will have to get past us. It won't be easy for any team to take the cup away.

That I can guarantee. . . .